Index

<u>Chapter 1:</u>
Sin Entered Into The World

Chapter 1:
"Sin Entered Into The World"
(1-A)

One of the most controversial stories in the bible is the story of Adam and Eve. Over the years, tradition has taught us so many varieties of what happened in the garden, but I am going to show you the revelation of the truth based completely off of the word of God.

First of all, we need to realize that Adam was type and shadow of Christ. The book of Romans is full of comparisons of the two.

Romans 5:14 says, *"Nevertheless, death reigned from Adam to Moses, even over them that had not sinned after the similitude of Adam's transgression, who is the figure of him that was to come."*

The original plan that God intended for Adam was carried out through Christ, but to truly understand why Jesus came, we must first understand what happened with Adam in the beginning.

<u>The Entrance of Sin</u>

Romans 5:12 says, *"Wherefore, as by one man, sin entered into the world, and death by sin; and so death passed upon all men, for that all have sinned."*

So here we see that sin entered into the world, but if you start to use your natural mind, you'll think he was talking about the planet.

Truthfully, when sin entered into the world, it wasn't the planet that the bible was referring to, it was Adam's heart.

It's not what goes into a man's heart that defiles him (Mark 7:14-23), so this easily disproves the theory of Adam and Eve eating an apple, or some other random fruit.

In fact, the bible never referred to an apple or any type of physical fruit when explaining the fall of man. So where did we get that from?

Yet, so many people today will defend their religion and traditions, not realizing that they are doing the very same thing Eve had done…believing a lie.

So what was the lie that Eve believed? I'm glad you asked!

Eve had been created from Adam to

help him in the garden (Genesis 2:22), so we know she was already made perfect and wise.

However, God commanded them not to eat from the tree of the knowledge of good and evil, but the devil "caused" her to believe that God was lying to them (Genesis 3:5).

Keep in mind, the devil did not force her to believe his lie. Her act to believe his lie and then to disobey God came of her own free will.

Out of Eve's own free will and curiosity, she believed a lie. The devil's lie seemed so good to her ears that she went back and shared it with Adam, who also believed (Genesis 3:6).

So you see, sin entered into the world when they ate of the lie, not some glossy apple.

The bible says that after they ate (believed), their eyes were opened. Now, we know he isn't talking about their natural eyes, because then that would mean they were blind up until that point. So you must break your traditional way of thinking.

The lie that was in the devil's heart entered into Eve's heart when she believed him. The same goes for Adam, who also believed it.

This is why the bible is so strict about us allowing just anything into our hearts as Christians, because evil communications corrupts good manners (I Corinthians 15:33). Here's an example…

How many people do you know right now that you can't even converse with, because all they do is complain about what's going wrong in their lives? All they needed to hear was that the boss was firing employees and now here you are, complaining with them.

Just because it may happen to someone else, doesn't mean it'll happen to you. Don't be so quick to believe what people say, because only God's word is final and people aren't God.

Offences of the Heart

It's very important that we learn to guard our hearts, because what we allow into it can change us completely, just as we seen with Adam.

When we first started the chapter, we began with Romans 5. Here, the bible used a couple of words that we are going to break down for you.

One is the word Sinned, the other is the word Offence. So, what do these words mean?

Sinned: *To disobey God's covenant; to miss the mark; to fall short of God's standard/righteousness; a voluntary transgression of a divine command of God;*
Offence: *it is the transgression of the law; a stumbling block that leads others into error;*

When Adam committed his offence of disobedience, he led everyone after him into error, or sin.

We usually tend to think that we are the ones who committed sin, but we never had the law. This is why we can come to appreciate the purpose for the death of Christ, because by his blood, we have all been saved by grace.

Romans 4:15 says, *"Because the law worketh wrath: for where no law is, there is no transgression."*

Now, although we have been saved from transgressions, sin still resides in a man's heart. Only the word can clean a man's heart from sin.

When you open your heart to information, you receive it. Rather it comes from God or man. You cannot receive or believe information unless you open your heart to it.

Proverbs 4:23 says, *"Keep thy heart with all diligence; for out of it are the issues of life."*

So who exactly are we keeping our hearts secured from?

Strange & Foolish Women

Now, before you take this literal and run with it, you must see this in the spirit, not the natural.

Foolish women aren't the type of silly women that you see every day. Instead, the bible is referring to the many foolish churches that you may visit. Either the preaching that you hear will be of the truth, or you will sit there and believe a lie.

If you follow the book of proverbs, you'll see how Solomon is very descriptive in showing you how to keep wisdom and understanding close to your heart, so that you don't fall for the deception of this world. However, what you may not have noticed is that he learned from experience.

Solomon wasn't always wise. In fact, the bible said that he loved many strange women (I Kings 11:1-4). They turned his heart from God, just as churches today do their members.

If a man teaches you from his flesh, it's not the word. The sad thing is, people believe anything a reverend says, not realizing that it's not the word.

One scripture and a bunch of talking will not get you delivered, but most people don't care.

People have believed a lie for so long, they don't want the truth. They only want you to tell them what they want to hear, so they can say "they went to church and had a good time". This is not enough and it's unacceptable.

When preachers aren't preaching the word of God, they'll always condemn you on what you wear, what you eat and more. They preach from the law, not from grace. These are the churches that you'd do well to avoid!

The wisdom of God is pure, peaceable, gentle, easy to be entreated, full of mercy and good fruits, without partiality and hypocrisy (James 3:17).

Those that preach from the wisdom of God should be able to show you in the bible where God said it. If they can't, do you really need more evidence?

The only sure way to know if a man is who he claims will only come by observing his fruit.

A good tree cannot bring forth evil fruit (Matthew 7:15-20), so before you start believing the man behind the pulpit, check his fruit!

As believers, we can't afford to believe everything that we hear, because wisdom enters through the heart, regardless if it's wisdom of God or of the world.

When true wisdom enters into your heart, its understanding will keep you (Proverbs 2:10-11).

I'm sure we've all heard at some point, a preacher telling us that the only way to be cleansed of our sins is through water baptism, but as we seen so far, sin resides in the heart. So how can we hope to wash our hearts through natural water?

The only way we can have our sins washed away is through the blood of Jesus. In fact, his entire mission to come into the flesh is completely tied into the original purpose of Adam, but we'll touch on that in a later chapter.

God's Garden

When we talk about comparisons to Adam and Christ, we find it here again in Genesis 2:15.

Adam was placed in the garden to keep the "garden". Jesus is accepted into our hearts to keep "us". What's the relation? We are not "in" God's garden, we ARE his garden (I Cor. 3:9).

Why do you think the bible tells us that we are known by our fruit? When we have Christ in our hearts, the fruits of the spirit are manifested in our lives. However, when we don't have Christ, our hearts are as a wasteland, a place where there is no fruit, only the works of the devil.

The saddest thing is that those who don't have Christ in their hearts actually think that they do and live in total denial…but if you truly have Christ in your garden, then the devil cannot operate through you.

Think about it, how can you come into a strong man's house and take his things, unless you first bind the strongman (Mark 3:27)?

This is what happened to Adam. When he believed a lie, he was put into bondage. He lost everything that God gave him, because he allowed the enemy to come in and take it.

His spiritual death came the same day he disobeyed God's direct command, causing him to fall from glory to the corruption of flesh.

It's easy to point fingers, but when we analyze his mistake, we can easily see the types and shadows of Christ and the church.

Now, although I'm saving this for a later chapter, I still want to show you a few things…

When Adam believed the lie, he did it for Eve's sake…just like when Christ came into the flesh and died, he did it for our sake.

You see, Adam was made perfect, but in order to understand Eve, he had to believe her. This is how he ate of the fruit.

Christ did the same for us, because he knew no sin, but was made sin for us, that we could be made the righteousness of God (2 Corinthians 5:21).

How does any of this affect me?

When Adam walked after the flesh, he died. When we walk after the flesh, we die as well. It's that simple.

Romans 8:13 says, *"For if ye live after the flesh, ye shall die: but if ye through the Spirit do mortify the deeds of the body, ye shall live."*

So how are we living after the flesh? It's through our carnal mind. When we do not control our fleshly desires, we allow the enemy to come in and corrupt our garden.

When you don't want to live for God, the information that you end up believing and receiving is the knowledge of the world. This fuels your carnal mind and will constantly fight against your spirit.

Knowing this, how can you ever recognize the truth if you're willing to listen and believe a lie?

Romans 8:6-8 says, *"To be carnally minded is death; but to be spiritually minded is life and peace. Because the carnal mind is enmity against God: for it is not subject to the law of God, neither indeed can be. So then they that are in the flesh cannot please God."*

Having carnality in the heart is what killed Adam. Christ came so that we would not have the same problem, but what good does it do if we still choose to willingly live by the flesh?

This is why so many Christians aren't reigning as God intended, because they chose to believe a lie.

Truth is, when you make the decision to live for God, the enemy will fight you, but regardless of how much stuff he tries to fill your head with, it can only take root when you believe it.

Galatians 5:17 says, *"For the flesh lusteth against the Spirit, and the Spirit against the flesh: and these are contrary the one to the other: so that ye cannot do the things that ye would."*

Keep this in mind, guaranteed life only comes from following Christ, but when you follow after your flesh, you will allow death to enter. So, if you can control the mind, you can control the man.

Even lust can be controlled, regardless of what you're lusting after or how bad you've got it…but you still have to want it. You can't feed your flesh all day long and complain when you don't see God operating in your life like he should.

God's grace isn't measured by who's in sin and who's not, because God has already forgiven you of the sins of Adam, but the works of the flesh is something you must put under on a daily basis. This will always be your battle until you learn to overcome it.

Adam's mistake was reversed when Jesus came into the flesh and died for all of mankind, but the choice to remain in sin is still ours and ours alone.

So will you follow after the truth, or will you believe a lie?

"Sin Entered Into The World"
(1-B)

In this chapter, we are going to go deeper into the examination of what the "World" really is. We've already explained that it referred to a man's flesh, but we really need to add more to your understanding.

The bible tells us not to love the world, nor the things that are in the world, because if we did, the love of the father is not inside of us (I John 2:15).

Well, how do I know if I'm in the world or not? I'm glad you asked!

The World

"For all that is in the world, the lust of the flesh, and the lust of the eyes, and the pride of life, is not of the Father, but is of the world. And the world passeth away, and the lust thereof: but he that doeth the will of God abideth forever." - I John 2:16-17.

Can you see why it is so important for us to do the will of God? When we operate in the flesh and fulfill our own desires, we only prove that the Father is not in us.

We are in the world, but we are not of it. The flesh can only dominate your heart when you operate with a carnal mind.

Remember when I touched on that in chapter 1-A? Your heart is a garden, but if you sow to the flesh, you'll only reap corruption (Gal. 6:8).

This is why you must renew your mind and die to your flesh daily, because God wants to see our lives prosper.

Romans 12:2 says, *"And be not conformed to this world: but be ye transformed by the renewing of your mind, that ye may prove what is that good, and acceptable, and perfect, will of God."*

The bible asks us not to be conformed to this world, yet we seem to continue living our lives as though we had never been redeemed. Why is that? It's because of the sin in our hearts.

When you come to church and go through the motions, you aren't really changing. Until Christ comes in and cleans your heart out, you'll never be able to retain the word.

Did you know that when Jesus came, his own people had no clue of who he was?

John 1:10 says, *"He was in the world,*

and the world was made by him, and the world knew him not. He came unto his own and his own received him not."

Think about that…what is it about a man that could make him blind to his own maker? It's his heart! If your heart is filled with sin, then your eyes are blinded to the truth.

The Heart

As you can see, we have covered a bit when concerning the heart. In fact, I promise you that this will not be the last time you'll hear about it.

The heart is the garden to which spiritual seeds are planted. However, the type of garden you might be growing just may be full of thorns and thistles…

Jeremiah 17:9 says, *"The heart is deceitful above all things, and desperately wicked: who can know it?"*

How can we pretend to be righteous, when our hearts are evil? If we never trust and allow Christ to come into our hearts and clean up our gardens, we'll find other places to put our trust…like, in man.

This is why there is a Jeremiah 17:5. It

is a direct statement from God to help clear up any confusion on where your trust should be.

It says, *"Thus saith the Lord; Cursed be the man that trusteth in man, and maketh flesh his arm, and whose heart departeth from the Lord. For he shall be like the heath in the desert, and shall not see when good cometh; but shall inhabit the parched places in the wilderness, in a salt land and not inhabited."*

So after reading that, why would you want to put your trust in man? God has spoken and told us what would happen when we do, yet we still disobey? Have you even noticed a pattern?

Adam did the exact same thing. God told him not to eat of the fruit from the tree, because he would die if he did (Genesis 2:17). Regardless, Adam still disobeyed God.

Can you now see how sin entered into the world? When we operate in the flesh, we allow ourselves to operate in the same disobedience that caused man to fall. This is why Christ came, so that we would no longer be forced to live after the flesh, but after the spirit.

For us to trust in anything but God,

shows the kind of heart we really have. Aren't you aware that you can't even be saved unless you trust in God?

It takes faith to have salvation, yet so many people would rather have more faith in their jobs to deposit their checks on Friday, then to trust God to save their souls from hell.

Why are our priorities so far off? Many of us would've never had to experience a broken heart if we would've kept our trust in God from the beginning, but some of us need to just learn the hard way.

The Cost Of His Disobedience

Did you know that when you live in sin, you are a servant of sin? It's only when you believe on Jesus that you can become one of his disciples (John 8:30). However, don't think you can have your cake and eat it, because either you will love one or hate the other, but you can't serve two masters.

Many of us knowingly live with disobedience in our hearts, but if we are disobedient, how can we truly be disciples of God?

Until we become born again, we are

still slaves to sin and with sin, comes consequences.

Adam's disobedience came because he believed his wife. Not God. His consequence? It cost him everything.

Genesis 3:17-19 says, *"And unto Adam he said, Because thou hast hearkened unto the voice of thy wife, and hast eaten of the tree, of which I commanded thee, saying Thou shalt not eat of it: cursed is the ground for thy sake; in sorrow shalt thou eat of it all the days of thy life; Thorns also and thistles shall it bring forth to thee; an thou shalt eat the herb of the field; In the sweat of thy face shalt thou eat bread, till thou return unto the ground; for out of it wast thou taken: for dust thou art, and unto dust shalt thou return."*

Now, after reading those scriptures, can you identify what his consequences were? Allow me to explain them for you.

First, the ground was cursed, growing thorns and thistles, causing him to no longer eat the fruit of therein, but instead to forever eat of his sorrows.

Now, because we know that sorrow isn't a physical fruit, this again should easily disprove the theory of an apple. That's not even scripture, no matter how many ministers attempt to back it up!

Second, because Adam sinned, he no longer shared the inheritance of righteousness. Instead, he had to work from the sweat of his brow to find food to eat. Can you start to see how he lost the dominion he once had?

Everything that happened to Adam must be understood in the spirit. You can't take your natural mind and try to figure it out, because you'll miss what God was trying to show you.

We learned in chapter 1-A, that Adam was type and shadow of Jesus Christ. The world is the flesh that we have and our heart is represented as the garden.

When Adam sinned, he was kicked out of the garden, not the world. So when God cursed the ground, it was the heart that was cursed. Now, because of the thorns and thistles, he was no longer able to eat of the fruit of his heart, but of the sorrows.

Well, if eating is interpreted as believing, then Adam was forced to live with the regret of his errors for the rest of his life.

The inheritance and dominion that he was once given in Genesis 1:28 would never be restored.

When a child is born, he is born into the same curse of Adam. It's only when that child becomes of age that he is responsible for what he knows. That child will grow up, automatically installed with a sinful nature (Ephesians 2:1-3).

Think about it, have you ever realized why little Johnny is so hardheaded? He was born into sin, just as we once were. Only salvation by grace can erase away that sinful nature (Ephesians 2:5).

The 4 Conditions of the Heart

We may not be aware of it, but we eat from our hearts every day. Every single time we open our mouth and say what we can or can't do, it is then brought into existence of our reality.

This is how we eat from our heart, because out of the abundance of the heart, the mouth speaks (Luke 6:45).

Proverbs 18:20-21 says, *"A man's belly shall be satisfied with the fruit of his mouth; and with the increase of his lips shall he be filled. Death and life are in the power of the tongue: and they that love it shall eat the fruit thereof."*

Did the bible just say that if you love what you say, you'll eat the fruit of it? This is powerful, because the ungodly will always have limits. Christians do not. But because we love to be like the ungodly, we suffer the same consequences as them.

It's easy to blame God when our lives don't prosper, but we fail to examine our own hearts. Our poor desire for the word is only proof that our gardens are full of thorns and thistles.

So what does thorns and thistles have to do with our hearts? Well, you couldn't have asked a better question!

In Luke 6:4-15, Jesus spoke a parable about the seed and the sower. The sower went out to sow seeds and some fell by the way side. Some fell by the rocks, some fell among thorns and the rest fell upon good ground.

The bible says that the thorns sprang up with the harvest and choked it, but the one's that fell on good ground, sprung up and produced fruit. His disciples couldn't understand the parable, but there's a reason for that.

We are given the mysteries of the kingdom, but others will only see parables, because they do not have the wisdom of God to understand them (Luke 8:10).

So when you sit through church, just look around…the ones that are sleep, tuned out and playing through the service are the ones who only hear parables. Their lives will never change.

Jesus explained his parable to them in Luke 8:11-15, so I'm going to show you exactly how he said it, word for word…so pay attention!

"Now the parable is this: **The seed** *is the word of God.* **Those by the way side** *are they that hear; then cometh the devil, and taketh away the word out of their hearts, lest they should believe and be saved.*

They on the rocks *are they, which, when they hear, receive the word with joy; and these have no root, which for a while believe, and in time of temptation fall away.*

And **that which fell among thorns** *are they, which, when they have heard, go forth, and are choked with cares and riches and pleasures of this life, and bring no fruit to perfection.*

But **that on the good ground** *are they, which in an honest and good heart, having heard the word, keep it, and bring forth fruit* *with patience."*

Did you get that? Before we head into the next chapter, I really want to break this down, because it's important that you understand this parable.

Think of this parable as though if God was talking about your church. Your pastor preached the word to everyone that was there and those that heard it were broken up into four categories.

Do you think you can be honest enough with yourself to find out where you fit?

The Seed:

This is the word. When you go and sit under a man of God, he plants the word into your heart. Your heart is the garden and the man of God is the sower.

It is very important that you find a true man of God, because if you sit under a false prophet, or even just settle for a church because your grandmother used to go there, you'll be given corrupt seeds that'll never bring forth fruit…even if your heart is the perfect garden.

When a disciple is made perfect, he'll be just like his master (Luke 6:40). So make sure you're being taught the true word of God and not from some preacher who ministers from his flesh.

Those by the Way Side:
As the bible said, these are the people who come to church, hear the word, but allow the devil to take what they just heard.

These are the same people who want to live a better life in Christ, but can't let their sinful ways go. Sometimes they will, sometimes they won't. Truth is, there's no consistency.

This is how the devil takes the word from them, because they gave him place in their daily lifestyles.

Do you give place to the devil? Well, if you were empowered on Sunday, but depleted by Wednesday…then this may just be you.

Those on the Rocks:
These are the people who appear to live righteous lives as long as nothing ever goes wrong. You know the ones who "lay their religion down" when they get talked about or confronted.

The bible say that they have no root

and all is well until temptation comes around, then they're the first ones to leave the church.

Those among Thorns:

These are the people that come to church, hear a few messages and think they're called to ministry, because the money is better than their original nine-to-five.

The bible says that they have no fruit, which means their new church never grows, or if it does, lives are not changing and hearts are not being delivered.

Those on Good Ground:

These are the people who hear the word and live by it. Their hearts receive the word with gladness. The bible says that they hear the word, keep it and the fruit becomes evident as they grow.

These are the ones who hear the word on Sunday, then buy the CD's afterwards so that they can hear it throughout the week.

Out of curiosity, when was the last time you bought a tape or CD of the service? When was the last time you actually listened to it?

Truth is, at first glance, everyone wants the word, but because their hearts are filled with darkness and thorns, they can't retain it.

The whole purpose you listen to the word throughout the week is so that you can water the seeds that were planted.

This is why so many people never see the Lord operate in their lives, because they absorb more music and television then they do the word…not realizing that it's causing your soil to dry up.

So many people now have no idea what their purpose is in this life, but it's only the lack of the word that makes you void of purpose and understanding.

The enemy knows this, that's why is so much easier to live in sin, because it's our original nature. You can't please God in the flesh, no matter what you've been told. Adam couldn't do it, neither can you!

The only way you'll ever be able to truly live, is to mortify the deeds of your body (Romans 8:13).

"Sin Entered Into The World"
(1-C)

When we read about Adam, we usually only retain information from the highlights of the story, such as the man, the woman, the tree and the snake...but if you've been reading this book so far, you know better!

We have been taught for years that the devil was a snake that lived in the garden, who then later deceived Eve. Really?

When you hear people repeat that version of the story, you should just shake your head in discontent.

People that only preach the surface of the word are void of understanding and will always see the deeper things of God as a mystery.

We learned earlier that the word must be revealed to you, otherwise you'll just perceive it as a parable. No one can truly understand a parable unless it's revealed.

The revelation of the mystery was given to one man in the New Testament, Paul the Apostle, because his revelation came from the Holy Ghost...wait, the same Holy

Ghost inside of you? We'll dig into that a bit later.

Look, the devil wasn't a slithering snake that was wrapped around the tree in the garden, although most people portray it that way. Instead, he approached her as an angel of light.

2 Corinthians 11:14 says, *"And no marvel; for Satan himself is transformed into an angel of light."*

The bible referred to him as the serpent, because of his cunningness. God even asks us to be wise as serpents, but humble as doves.

Are you ready for another jaw-dropper? The devil wasn't in the garden before he beguiled Eve, he came from the field and THEN into the Garden of Eden (Genesis 3:1).

When we look at this through our spiritual lenses, we'll see that the serpent was a false prophet who knew the word, but corrupted it and fed it to anyone that would believe it.

2 Corinthians 11:13 says, *"For such are false apostles, deceitful workers, transforming themselves into an angel of light."*

These are the same men that Jesus called out in Matthew. He called them a generation of vipers, because they spoke a corrupted word.

These men had evil in their hearts, but we've learned so far that out of the abundance of the heart, the mouth speaks (Matt.12:34).

So now that we understand where he came from, we need to now see why he came.

The Temptations

When the devil came to Eve, he tempted her. He didn't have any power or control until Adam allowed him to have it. He knew he couldn't deceive Adam, so he used Eve.

Remember how we just read about false prophets in 2 Corinthians? This is exactly what happened with Eve...

First, the devil challenged her intelligence by asking her, "Hath God said?" Then, when he seen that she wavered, he tempted her.

If you remember what you read a few pages ago, you'll see that Eve's heart represents those by the way side, because she had the word, but she allowed the enemy to come in and take it.

Although she was already like God, she allowed pride to push her into thinking she could be a god. Then later, she seen that lie to be good for food, because she wanted to believe it. This is how it became pleasing to the eyes. She later then ate of it.

Do you see what just happened? The devil hit her with a three-piece and a biscuit! He tempted her with the lust of the flesh, the lust of the eyes and the pride of life. How? Let's examine that…

Lust of the flesh: The lie that she heard cause her to want to eat of it, because she seen that it was good for food (Genesis 3:6).

Lust of the Eyes: She had seen that it was pleasant to the eyes, which was the desire to believe it (Genesis 3:6).

The Pride of Life: She was told that her eyes would be open and that she could be as a god herself (Genesis 3:5).

I John 2:16 says, *"For all that is in the world, the lust of the flesh, and the lust of the eyes, and the pride of life, is not of the Father, but is of the world."*

The only way the devil could've gotten Eve to sin, he had to see if she truly believed what God had said. Remember, it was only when she wavered when he began to tempt her.

The devil even tried the same tricks on Jesus in Matthew 4, but Jesus never wavered in what he believed. Instead, he quoted the word, because he knew who he was.

Let's compare his temptations with Eve's…

Lust of the Flesh: The devil tempted Jesus with food, because he knew Jesus had grew hungry from fasting in the wilderness. He asked him to turn stones to bread, but Jesus quoted the word instead (Matthew 4:3-4).

Lust of the Eyes: Jesus was taken up to the holy city and sat on a pinnacle of the temple. The devil asked him to cast himself down so that he could see his angels come to his rescue, but he rebuked the devil again with the word (Matthew 4:5-7).

The Pride of Life: Jesus was then taken up to a high mountain, so that he could see all of the kingdoms of the world.

The devil was willing to give him all of it, if he were to fall down and worship him…but we know the devil was crazy for that one, because he was instantly rebuked and sent away (Matthew 4:8-10).

It's very important that you realize the devil's purpose for the temptations, because if you don't, you'll fall for one of his tricks and not even know it.

The devil was once an angel of God, but was cast out of heaven because he had a corrupt heart.

Pride entered into his heart, causing him to want to be like God (Isaiah 14:12-15).

Just as you seen with Eve, all the way to Jesus, his tricks have never changed. Why? It's because that's what was in his heart.

He couldn't have everything that he wanted on his own, so he tried to take it from the ones who had it.

He went after Adam. He went after Jesus. Now, he's after us. However, the power that he took from Adam, Jesus took it from him. So he has no power, just like in the beginning…until you give it to him.

We are to give no place to the devil (Ephesians 4:27), but when we operate in the flesh, we open the door for him to come in.

He only wants to use you, because you

were given what he always wanted. Power and authority. It's just sad, because most Christians don't even know what they have inherited through salvation.

Satan doesn't go after those in the world, because they have no power and no future. Instead, he targets the church, but his desires can only be manifested through us when we operate in the flesh, not when we are in Christ.

A New Man

2 Corinthians 5:17 says, *"Therefore if any man be in Christ, he is a new creature: Old things are passed away; behold, all things are become new."*

Well, how are we put into Christ? We are put into Christ through salvation. When you walk up to that altar and receive Christ, your old heart is replaced with a new one. Now you have a restored garden that can bring forth fruit.

When a man receives salvation, the old world passes away (which is the old man), then all becomes new, which means he can now do the will of God. But what exactly is the will of God?

It's simple, the will of God is for us to believe on his son, Jesus (John 6:40). However, when you don't receive salvation, you'll have strong desires of the flesh, that'll keep your heart from baring fruit.

When you come into Christ, everything changes. Rather than having the lust of the flesh, you'll mortify the deeds of your body.

Rather than having the lust of the eyes, your perspective changes to only see as Christ sees and rather than having pride, the Lord replaces it with faith in him.

When you change, people aren't supposed to see the same person they once knew. Just ask yourselves, are you the same person you were last year?

2 Corinthians 5:16 says, *"Wherefore henceforth know we no man after the flesh: yea, though we have known Christ after the flesh, yet now henceforth know we him no more."*

Translation: We can't see each other after the flesh, because we are now in Christ, and Even though Jesus himself was here in flesh, we can't continue to see him as "Baby Jesus", or anything else when using our carnal minds.

When Jesus came in the world, he came to start a new generation. Everyone that came after Adam were born into sin and under the law. These are the generation(s) of Adam (Genesis 5:1).

In Adam, all died, but in Christ, all are made alive. Everyone that came after Jesus has the opportunity to be placed in the generation (or the kingdom) of Christ (Matthew 1:1).

Our perspective should be looking unto Jesus, who is the author and the finisher of our faith. This controls the lust of the eyes, because if we are seeking first his kingdom, then everything we need will be added to us anyway (Matthew 6:33).

You see, Adam operated in the kingdom until he believed a lie. It wasn't that he felt bad and left the kingdom, he and his wife were put out (Genesis 3:23). So why is it that so many church folk find the kingdom, then feel they need to leave?

Trees do not uproot themselves and go from location to location. They remain where they are placed and endure the storms. So why is it that we feel the need to uproot ourselves? It's because our hearts haven't truly been renewed.

Some church folk just don't want the word. It's that simple. They don't want to remain in a word-preaching church, because they want to be somewhere where their flesh can rise.

What are these places? These are places where they can hear a scripture, sing, dance and go home, without any obligation to change.

A place where they aren't held accountable for their actions, because it's good enough to just say "I went to church today".

Remember when we talked about the seed and the sower, these people are those on the rocks. As soon as they are offended, they'll leave and just find another church. They have no allegiance and no roots.

Truth is, no matter how bitter, or how hard your heart is, once you give your life over to Christ, he will give you a new heart.

Ezekiel 11:19-20 says, *"And I will give them one heart, and I will put a new spirit within you; and I will take the stony heart out of their flesh, and will give them an heart of flesh: That they may walk in my statutes, and keep mine ordinances, and do them: and they shall be my people, and I will be their God.*"

"Sin Entered Into The World"
(1-D)

So far, we've covered many issues of the heart that shows a comparison between a pure heart and a corrupt heart.

We've learned that a pure heart is what the bible called, "Good Ground" and a corrupt heart is clearly the opposite.

When we hear the word preached and reject it, the word never takes root and we never produce fruit.

This is because the ground is cursed and need to be restored. Now, although we know that the ground is the heart, we're going to take a quick look at the word "Curse" and "Cursed".

Cursed: *condemned; corrupted; to make powerless; unable to bring forth fruit; bound; to withhold the blessings/wealth and position of sonship; the disfavor of God; doomed for punishment;*

Curse: *to condemn; the judicial act of declaring one guilty*

When Adam sinned, he was declared

guilty, so God cursed the ground, separating Adam from the garden. It's a powerful thing to allow sin to separate you from God, because nothing can separate you from God but sin.

Isaiah 59:2 says, *"But your iniquities have separated between you and your God, and your sins have hid his face from you, that he will not hear."*

Did you know that you can't even get a prayer through to God when you are still in sin?

He hides his face from sin, so if we say we are Christians, then why do we try to fit in and act as the world?

We don't think we're in sin, but until we receive salvation and have our hearts renewed, he will only see the sins of Adam in us, because by one man's disobedience, all were made sinners (Romans 5:19).

Think about it, how many times have you prayed and never got an answer? Truth is, God will not forsake his own. So rather than allowing pride to tell you that you're saved anyway, let God take your heart and give you a new one.

Condemnation

When a person is cursed they have already been condemned, but Jesus came not to condemn the world, but to save it (John 3:17).

Until a person receives Christ, they are still cursed. However, when God saves you, no man can curse you from that point forward.

Remember the lady that was caught in the act of adultery? Well, we'll use her for an example...

If you've never heard the story before, it takes place in John 8. It's a story of how the scribes and Pharisees brought a woman before Jesus because they wanted to catch him in a lie.

Jesus had already said that he came to save the world and not to condemn it, but when they found a woman who was "caught in the act" of adultery, they wanted to see if Jesus would obey the law and condemn her...all while knowing he'd be contradicting himself at the same time.

Jesus had seen through their deception and told them if they were without sin, then they could stone her (John 8:7). However, because they knew they weren't sinless, they walked away.

John 8:10-11 says, *"When Jesus had lifted up himself, and saw none but the woman, he said unto her, Woman, where are those thine accusers? Hath no man condemned thee? She said, no man, Lord. And Jesus said unto her, Neither do I condemn thee: go, and sin no more."*

You see that? There were no one left to accuse her, because God had already forgiven her.

He has done the same thing with us, but he also told her to go and sin no more. Why? Because it was sin that got her in trouble in the first place.

The scribes and Pharisees were religious leaders. In other words, they were church folk. Without saying too much, I'm sure we all know that no one can condemn you like religious church folk.

Here's the part that I don't want you to miss…when Jesus requested the religious leaders to stone her if they were without sin, they walked away. Why would they do that? It's simple. They still had sin in their hearts and they knew it.

When you operate under the law,

you're only justified through self-righteousness, which makes you feel like going to church is enough. You'll always see other people's fault instead of your own.

This is the spirit of condemnation. Just like thorns and thistles, it grows deep into a man's heart when his heart is not renewed through salvation.

One of the biggest issues in the church today is that most preachers only preach the law, not realizing that they are preaching condemnation.

If you read Proverbs 23:1-12, it'll warn you not to eat and absorb the fruit of the wicked. Verse 3 says to not be desirous of deceitful meat.

So when you hear a preacher telling you what God said, be sure he can back it up by the word, otherwise he's just preaching from his flesh.

The Imagination

A few pages ago, we went over the way the devil tricked Eve. First he challenged her intelligence, but then once he realized that she wavered in what she believed, he tricked her.

We also realized "why" he did it. He wanted both the power and the authority that was given to Adam, but he couldn't just walk up to Adam and take it. Instead, he planted the seeds of his desires into Eve.

Adam and Eve were in the kingdom of God, just as we are today. They had the power to bring their imaginations to life, just as we can right now. This is how we eat from our hearts, because life and death are in the power of the tongue.

When we confess life and prosperity over our lives, we bare the fruits of life and prosperity. When we confess sickness and death, we bring it to pass as well.

The devil knew all of this, that's why he had caused Eve to believe his lie. He could not bring anything to pass on his own, but she could. All she needed was his image in her heart for her to speak his desires into reality.

Do you not realize the powers you inherit when you receive Christ? The devil knows, but he'll do whatever he can to keep you from realizing it, because an ineffective Christian is just as harmless as an unbeliever.

Once we take hold of an idea, we can birth it out by the words of our mouth. Do you now see why it's so important to guard your heart?

You can't sit up and watch the news all day, hearing how bad the economy is, because the "Just" shall live by faith. But what happens is that Christians see the news and panic, causing them to waver in their beliefs.

Once this does happens, you have successfully planted the seeds of the devil into your heart. He already challenged your intelligence, but your wavering proved that you don't know the word like you should.

Then, he comes in and tell you all of the bad that's about to happen. We believe it (which is eating the fruit of his lie), then turn around and speak it to our lives.

Have you ever heard someone say, "Girl, this economy is bad!" or, "I don't know how I'm gonna make it…"

Don't you realize that life and death is in the power of your tongue? Sure the economy may go bad, but that isn't supposed to affect the church. We are supposed to remain fruitful, even in the times of famine, but because you believed a lie, you have to now eat from it.

Regardless of how bad things look on

the outside, you must never lose confidence in Christ. He will always provide a way of escape when you are tempted (1 Corinthians 10:13).

Anything that comes into your mind that does not line up with what God said is proof that the devil is searching for a spot to plant his seeds. So when you start to think on the negative, cast those sinful thoughts and imaginations down.

2 Corinthians 10:4-5 says, *"For the weapons of our warfare are not carnal, but mighty through God to the pulling down of strong holds; Casting down imaginations, and every high thing that exalteth itself against the knowledge of God, and bringing into captivity every thought to the obedience of Christ."*

Passing Away

When you come into the kingdom of Christ, the change in your heart will be evident, because the old nature you once had will pass away.

This is what the scriptures mean when it reads about a new heaven and a new earth (Matthew 24:35), because once you receive

Christ, your old earth passes away.

You do remember what the earth is, right? Exactly, it's your heart!

Revelation 21:1 says, *"And I saw a new heaven and a new earth: for the first heaven and the first earth were passed away; and there was no more sea."*

The old heaven and earth referred here is the sinful nature, the carnal mind and the fleshly desires that we inherited from Adam.

The sea is represented as the wavering that tosses you to and fro. It's the doubt in a man's heart, but we'll deal with this more in depth in a later chapter.

Once we receive Christ, he washes it all away and a gives us a new life.

Verse 2 says, *"And I John saw the holy city, new Jerusalem, coming down from God out of heaven, prepared as a bride adorned for her husband."*

Now, you can't use your natural mind on this, because if you did, you'd get confused on how a city would come out of heaven.

As the church, we are the New Jerusalem. Remember how you just read about the new generation of Christ? It's you and me.

Verses 3-4 says, *"And I heard a great voice out of heaven saying, Behold, the tabernacle of God is the men, and he will dwell with the, and they shall be his people, and God himself shall be with them, and be their God. And God shall wipe away all tears from their eyes; and there shall be no more death, neither shall there be any more pain: for the former things are passed away."*

Keep in mind, those who only read the surface of the word will try and tell you that the scriptures you just read hasn't happened yet...really?

Are you saying that I have to wait until sometime in the future before I receive a new heaven and a new earth?

Tradition teaches the deep things of God all wrong, because they only see them as parables. Remember when we talked about the generation of Jesus versus the generation of Adam?

Until Jesus died for our sins, he clearly told us that the generation of Adam would not pass until everything he said was fulfilled (Matthew 24:34). Then in John 19:30, he said, *"It is finished"*.

Chapter 2:
Death Entered Into The World

Chapter 2:
"Death Entered Into The World"
(2-A)

When Adam sinned, sin entered into the world. We've covered a lot of ground so far, so I hope you've been following closely.

Now, I'm going to show you that when Adam sinned, Death entered into the world as well.

Romans 5:12 says, *"Wherefore, as by one man sin entered into the world, and death by sin; and so death passed upon all men for that all have sinned."*

It's important for you to understand that sin and death is not the devil. How do we know? Because although the devil entered into the garden, sin and death could not come until Adam believed a lie.

This is powerful, because sin and death were never meant to enter the garden. Adam was created and placed in the garden to keep it (Gen. 2:15), but failed his duty when he let his guard down (Genesis 3:6).

As I showed you earlier, Christ was faced with the exact same temptations as Adam, but we need to see just how accurate the comparison is.

The Garden Comparison

When Christ went to pray, the devil came into the garden of Gethsemane, but he used Judas. His disciples were told to keep watch (Mark 14:34).

However, they kept falling asleep and when they finally awoken, Judas had entered the garden and betrayed Jesus.

Mark 14:41-42 says, *"And he cometh the third time, and saith unto them, Sleep on now, and take your rest: It is enough, the Son of man is betrayed into the hands of sinners. Rise up, let us go; lo, he that betrayed me is at hand."*

So here, we see that Peter, James and John had failed their mission. Jesus commanded that they watch, but their flesh was too weak to pray.

Okay, I need you to put your thinking caps on for a minute…

We all know how strong the flesh is, because the bible tells us to die to it daily. Well, if that's the case, how is it that the flesh was so weak all of a sudden? The flesh wasn't weak until it came down time to pray.

It's almost like the flesh was throwing a temper tantrum, because he was being forced to do something he didn't want to do.

Be sure to keep this in mind…the flesh will always go against what God wants you to do. Always.

Deceived?

If we continue to see the comparisons between Christ and Adam, we'll see that although Adam sinned, he was not deceived. How do we know this? Because Christ can't be tempted with evil (James 1:13).

1 Timothy 2:14 says, *"And Adam was not deceived, but the woman being deceived was in the transgression."*

Adam took on her sin so that he could be with her, just as Christ took on our sins so that we could be with him (Galatians 1:4).

When we evaluate the differences between the two, we'll see that Adam's sin guaranteed that we'd all die, but Christ came and died in our place so that we could live forever.

Isn't that amazing? It's just sad when you spend all of your years on Earth and never choose life. Death was never a choice, it was automatically guaranteed.

This is why we should appreciate Christ even more, because he came to save us, even though he knew we were sinners (1 Timothy 1:15).

John 1:10-13 says, *"He was in the world, and the world was made by him, and the world knew him not. He came unto his own, and his own received him not. But as many as received him, to them gave he power to become the sons of God, even to them that believe on his name: Which were born, not of blood, nor of the will of the flesh, nor of the will of man, but of God."*

"Death Entered Into The World"
(2-B)

Earlier we went over the three temptations that the enemy uses to cause us to fall into sin, which was the lust of the flesh, lust of the eyes and the pride of life.

However, we also learned that when lust is conceived, it brings forth sin, which then brings forth death (James 1:15). So death is the end result of lust? Yes!

This is why the enemy used his three temptations on Adam, then on Jesus and now on us. If we allow ourselves to give in to lust, we'll find ourselves in sin. Once we do, death is inevitable.

All souls belong to God and if you read Ezekiel 18:4, you'll see that the soul that sinneth will die. If you noticed, Eve was a representation of Adam's soul.

We've talked about death, but there are three types of deaths that a man can experience. We'll explain it all in a later chapter, but I want to first touch on it a bit here.

One is a **Spiritual death**, which is separation from God. When a man is not saved, he is already dead. Only when Christ enters his heart can a man be made alive.

Next, is the **Physical death**. From dust thou art and to dust thou shalt return (Genesis 3:19).

One day, your body will die and return the ground, but if you are in Christ when your body dies, you're promised a glorified body.

Last, we have **Eternal death**. If you suffer a physical death before you accept Christ, you will forever be cut off from God.

There will be no chance to be made alive in Christ, because that choice is only available to those who have not yet suffered a physical death.

It is only appointed unto men once to die (Hebrews 9:27), so either you will die to your flesh, or you will die an eternal death.

There is no misunderstanding with this, because the bible is very black and white when it comes to life and death.

We don't realize it, but not controlling our lust is what leads us into sin. Once our sin is committed, death comes. After seeing this, how can you continue to feed into your lust when it will only bring you closer to death?

You can never learn to control the sinful nature in your life if you never learn to control the lusts in your flesh. This is where it all starts.

LUST

"Let no man say when he is tempted, I am tempted of God: for God cannot be tempted with evil, neither tempteth he any man: But every man is tempted, when he is drawn away of his own lust, and enticed. Then when lust hath conceived, it bringeth forth sin: and sin, when it is finished, bringeth forth death." - James 1:13-15.

As you can see, our temptations come when we are drawn away by our own lusts. This is what happened to Eve in the garden, because she desired the fruit that was said to make one wise.

Once lust was conceived, it caused her and Adam to sin. Their sin caused their eyes to be opened, which is where death came in.

Now, they were forced to suffer a spiritual death, which we just learned is to be cut off from God.

Lust will keep you from obeying God, because the flesh fights against the spirit, as do the spirit against the flesh.

Galatians 5:17 says, *"This I say then, Walk in the Spirit, and ye shall not fulfill the lust of the flesh. For the flesh lusteth against the Spirit, and the Spirit against the flesh: and these are contrary the one to the other: so that ye cannot do the things that ye would. But if ye be led of the Spirit, ye are not under the law."*

When you go out into public and see a beautiful man or woman, it's natural to look. We are all made in God's image and his likeness. God is a beautiful being.

My wife is a beautiful woman, so I know other Christian men from the church will look. Again, that's natural…but when you look with the desire to want more, lust will enter your heart. Regardless of the person you're looking at.

It's at this stage where you are the most vulnerable, because now that the desire and lust is there, coursing through your veins. All they have to do is ask you out to dinner and you'll be one drink away from coming out of your drawers! It's sad, but very true.

Unless it's a case of rape, you can never willingly lie down and have sex with someone that you never had a sexual desire for. Your flesh has to want it to some degree.

That one night of sin was given birth and conceived from the lust that you allowed into your heart from earlier.

The Law of Sin

We must understand that we will always be tempted of sin when we remain under the law. Since the law tells you what you can and can't do, it's guaranteed that we'd break it, making us disobedient.

Romans 7:7-8 says, *"What shall we say then? Is the law sin? God forbid. Nay, I had not known sin, but by the law: for I had not known lust, except the law had said, Thou shalt not covet. But sin, taking occasion by the commandment, wrought in me all manner of concupiscence. For without the law sin was dead."*

What those scriptures were saying is that we didn't even know what sin was, until there became a law against it. We didn't even know anything about lust, until the commandment told us not to do it. Had there of been no law, there would be no sin.

If you put your thinking caps on, you'll see that God gave Adam a commandment, not a choice. Adam was commanded to not eat of the tree. He wasn't given a choice to choose the one he wanted.

We know it was the devil that tempted Eve, not God. If you've been following along, you'll remember that God cannot be tempted, neither tempts he any man (James 1:13).

Because of Christ, we are no longer under the law, but of grace (Rom. 6:14). All we have to do is obey Christ and we will spend our days in prosperity. It's only when we disobey that we parish and die without knowledge (Job 36:11).

Isaiah 1:19 says, *"If ye be willing and obedient, ye shall eat the good of the land: But if ye refuse and rebel, ye shall be devoured with the sword: for the mouth of the Lord hath spoken it."*

It's amazing when you think about it, because if Adam had obeyed God, he'd be alive today. All he had to do was obey God? Well, how much different do you think it is with us?

Under the law, commandments had to be followed. Under grace, we are given a choice. We have to choose God's righteousness, not our own (Rom. 6:5-8).

Proverbs 14:12 says, *"There is a way which seemeth right unto a man, but the end thereof are the ways of death."*

So what is this saying? It's saying that you cannot rely on your carnal mind to get you anywhere with Christ. In fact, to operate with a carnal mind is to be spiritually dead. Allow me to show you...

The Carnal Mind and The Devourer

When we operate with a carnal mind, it shows that we are still in the flesh and not in the Spirit. The carnal mind isn't subject to the law of God.

Romans 8:6-8 says, *"For to be carnally minded is death; but to be spiritually minded is life and peace. Because the carnal mind is enmity against God: for it is not subject to the law of God, neither indeed can be. So then they that are in the flesh cannot please God."*

So we can't even please God when we use our carnal minds? This is interesting, because if we evaluate ourselves, are we really living lives that are pleasing to God, or are we just doing our own thing?

If you're willing to be honest, the

majority of us are doing our own thing, not realizing that when we operate in the flesh, we are giving place to the devil. The bible strictly tells us not to give place to the devil.

You see, the devil is as a roaring lion, walking about and seeing who he can devour (1 Peter 5:8), but not devour as in eating you up…let's be realistic here.

If you remember the parable of the seed and the sower, Jesus said that it was the enemy who comes in and devours the word from you.

When we hear the word, seeds are planted. If we operate in a carnal mind, the seeds will never take root anyway. The enemy doesn't want you to retain the word, because he needs a place to stay.

When Adam was created, he and Eve were supposed to resist the devil by being steadfast in the faith, which is all that God requires from us to keep the enemy at bay.

Remember, the devil couldn't have deceived Eve if she hadn't wavered in the faith she already had.

Many of us waver so much that we don't really know what we believe. This is how the enemy comes in and devour what we get, because our carnal minds keep us from understanding how to apply the word of God in our lives.

The Lord knew that the enemy would come in and try to corrupt your fruit, which is why he promised us that he would rebuke the devourer for our sake. All he's asking from us is that we remain steadfast in the faith.

Malachi 3:11 says, *"And I will rebuke the devourer for your sakes, and he shall not destroy the fruits of your ground; neither shall your vine cast her fruit before the time in the field, saith the Lord of hosts."*

Chapter 3:
Spiritual Death Entered Into The World

Chapter 3:
"Spiritual Death Entered Into The World"
(3-A)

The purpose of this chapter is to understand one of the trinities of death. If you can remember what we went over in the last chapter, you'll see that there is a natural death, an eternal death and the one we're going to touch on now, which is a spiritual death.

When a man is not born again, his soul is spiritually dead, separated from God, dead to God, cut off from God and still dead in his trespasses and sins (Eph. 2:1-10).

A man that is not born again still operates with the carnal mind, which means he can never understand the things of God, because the things of God can only be spiritually discerned.

1 Corinthians 2:14 says, *"But the natural man receiveth not the things of the Spirit of God: for they are foolishness unto him: nether can he know them, because they are spiritually discerned."*

Have you ever tried to speak to

someone about the word and they just couldn't comprehend what you're saying? It's because their carnal mind will not allow them to understand the things of the Spirit.

You'd be shocked at how many people leave church without an understanding, but feel at peace because they simply showed up for church.

One of the reasons that church folk can't comprehend the word is because they have been told a lie for so long, that they refuse to believe the truth when they hear it.

This is also why some may read this book and discard the information, because instead of agreeing with the word, they'd rather hold on to what they were taught in Sunday school as a kid.

What we need to realize is that when we stick to our traditions, rather than open our hearts to the truth, we remain under the law, which is our own righteousness.

Remember what we've learned about the law? It's the law that keeps us from grace (God's work on the cross).

Did you know when God placed Adam in the garden, that the law was already present (Genesis 2:15-17)?

Adam was already covered in grace,

but when he sinned, he was now under the law and realized he was naked (Gen. 3:6-11).

Adam was put out of the garden, losing all of his power and dominion. God said that the day he ate of the tree, that he should surely die, which is exactly what happened.

Adam's death wasn't a natural death, but a spiritual death. Once he was put out of the garden, he was cut off from God. When he once lived in the garden, God kept him. When he was put out, he had to keep himself (Genesis 2:19).

Can you see the comparisons between grace and the law? When you are under grace, the peace of God will keep your heart and mind (Philippians 4:6-7), but when you're under the works of the law, you have to keep your own heart and with all diligence (Proverbs 4:23).

This is where most Christians are, because although we are saved by grace, we still operate under the law. Why would you want that?

When it comes to the law, there's always something that has to be done on our part, but not with grace. All we had to do was accept it, because salvation is not something we work for, it was a gift (Romans 6:23).

Truly Blind?

Have you ever tried to witness to someone that knows everything? It's by far one of the most frustrating things to do. Why? Because it's like teaching a child to learn advanced chemistry.

If they think they already know it, they'll never really learn the right way, because pride allows them to think they're already right.

This is what happened to Jesus when he healed a blind man on the Sabbath day (Jn. 9). The Pharisees seen the miracles, yet they still wouldn't believe, because their main concern was that the law of the Sabbath was broken.

They couldn't see what God was doing, because they were the ones who were truly blind. The Jews upheld the law so intensely until they couldn't even believe that a man could be saved by grace alone.

John 9:39-41 says, *"And Jesus said, For judgment I am come into this world, that they which see not might see; and that they which see might be made blind. And some of the Pharisees which were with him heard these words, and said unto him, Are we blind also? Jesus said unto them, if ye were blind, ye should have no sin: but now ye say, We see; therefore your sin remained."*

Being spiritually dead is the same thing as being blind. You cannot see when you are dead, because there is no light, only darkness.

This is what it means to be born into sin, because we were already born dead.

Being born into sin isn't something we did, just like there is nothing we can do to be saved. Salvation is a gift and all we have to do is receive it. Once we do, we are then born into Christ.

The Publican & The Pharisee

Although grace through salvation is a gift, people still feel that what they've done is what makes them righteous…but that's not the case.

When we trust in our own works of righteousness, we discredit what Christ did on the cross. He died so that we could be made righteous through him, but people still think it's about what they've done.

Here, I'm going to show you a passage in Luke, where Jesus spoke a parable about a Publican and the Pharisee. Both were sinners who came to the temple to pray, but watch the difference in their attitudes…

Luke 18:11-12 says, *"The Pharisee stood and prayed thus with himself, God, I thank thee, that I am not as other men are, extortioners, unjust, adulterers, or even as this publican. I fast twice in the week, I give tithes of all that I possess."*

Now, right here you can clearly see that the Pharisee is stuck on himself. He comes into prayer, giving God his list of good deeds, but we know that's not what makes him righteous.

He even pointed out the publican in his prayer. Really? Can you really come before God flawless and without fault? Are your works enough to validate how perfect you are?

Luke 18:13-14 says, *"And the publican, standing afar off, would not lift up so much as his eyes unto heaven, but smote upon his breast, saying, God be merciful to me a sinner. I tell you, this man went down to his house justified rather than the other: for every one that exalteth himself shall be abased; and he that humbleth himself shall be exalted."*

So the publican was made justified instead of the perfect Pharisee? Yes.

The publican was a sinner and he knew it. He didn't try to be perfect or pretend to be something he wasn't. In fact, he couldn't even lift his head, because he knew he didn't belong in prayer...but his humility is what God wanted.

The Pharisee was just as much a sinner as the publican, but rather than admit that he was at fault, he threw his resume in God's face, showing how righteous he was, but how can you come to God already justified?

This is a lesson that we need to learn, because all God wants is for you to come before him as you are, which is without pride, but humility. When you come to God with your perfect resume, you will be turned away.

How many churches do you know that reminds you of the Pharisee in Jesus' parable? They brag about how much they give, they put everyone else down, because they feel no one else is really saved but them? This is operating under the law.

You may not attend such a church, but

is it possible that you may be a reflection of the Pharisee?

Do you look down on the same people you were commanded by God to help? At night when you go to bed, does your prayer consist of "Me, my four and no more", "Me, we and us three", or "Me, myself and I"?

Another Way?

I'm really stressing the fact that our righteousness isn't based off of anything that we've done, because as we've seen with the Pharisee and the publican, God abases such prideful behavior.

Over the years, I have ministered to many people, those who are here now and those who have gone on. One thing I have said to all of them is that once they learn the truth, do not allow yourself to believe a lie.

In the days of Adam, believing a lie cost him his kingdom, his dominion and his power. What makes you think it's any different now?

When you sit up in churches that do not preach the gospel, you're allowing yourself to be told a lie.

For example, when you go to churches

that teaches salvation through baptism, or that you're required to confess your sins to a natural man, you better run!

This may shock you, but it's essential for you to learn…God isn't forgiving sins anymore, because he already did it nearly 2000 years ago when he died for us!

So how are we in sin when we have been put into Christ? Is there sin in Christ?

No, but there is sin in the law, which is why church folk still think they need to ask for forgiveness.

This is how you can tell when a Christian is under the law and carnal minded, because they still feel like they have to do something to remain cool with God.

What can you possibly do? Didn't you just read about the Pharisee and the publican?

Our entire foundation of Christianity is based off of what Christ did. This is why it's called "Christianity", not "Ustianity".

If Jesus came and died for our sins already (1 Cor. 15:3), then why are we confessing our sins to a natural priest?

Just as any other pastor, bishop or prophet, the priest is a natural man. He also is born into sin as the rest of us, but if he doesn't believe the death, burial and resurrection, he's going to hell too! So how is he helping you do something that was already done?

Galatians 1:4 says, *"Who gave himself for our sins, that he might deliver us from this present evil world, according to the will of God and our Father."*

You see that? Keep in mind what the world is, do you remember? It's the flesh. There's no good thing in the flesh (Rom. 7:18), which is why Galatians called it evil, yet we tend to exalt our flesh as the Pharisee did.

This is what most people do, they discredit what God has done, because they feel as if it takes away their ability to do something more. But we are under grace now, there's nothing that we have to do.

Only the law requires you to "do something". Grace only requires that we do nothing but "believe".

When Jesus forgave us of our sins, he was paying a debt that we couldn't pay. When we continue to seek forgiveness, it's just like saying that he didn't do a good enough job at the cross.

If a priest can help you with forgiveness, then why do we need Jesus?

1 Peter 2:24 says, *"Who his own self bare our sins in his own body on the tree, that we, being dead to sins, should live unto righteousness: by whose stripes ye were healed."*

Jesus was beaten on the cross, yet by his stripes we are healed (Isaiah 53:5). All we have to do to receive healing is to just believe we're healed. That's it!

The same goes with our own salvation, so why are we being told that we can only be saved through water baptism?

Isn't that just natural water? How can our sins be washed away through natural water? If it could, we could just wash our own sins away, but don't you know that Jesus washed us from our sins in his own blood (Revelation 1:5)?

When Paul preached the gospel, his biggest enemy was the law. The people were so carnal minded, they tried to follow the works, rather than understand the gospel that he was preaching.

1 Corinthians 1:17 says, *"For Christ sent me not to baptize, but to preach the gospel: not with wisdom of words, lest the cross of Christ should be made of none effect. For the preaching of the cross is to them that*

perish foolishness; but unto us which are saved it is the power of God."

So what's the preaching of the cross? It's the gospel of salvation. His death on the cross is how we are dead to sins and made alive.

Remember, when you haven't received the gift of salvation, you are still spiritually dead.

When you are born again, there's a change in your nature. You are no longer under the sin of the law, but now you are saved by grace. Your sins are forgiven and remembered no more.

So you can't let a man tell you that you're still a sinner. Why, because you made a mistake? You are in Christ now. There is no sin in Christ, so there is no sin in you.

Here's why it's so hard for carnal minded people to accept that, because they still feel like they need to go to God in prayer and seek forgiveness. The only reason you'd need to still need to seek forgiveness is if you are still under the law.

Before Adam sinned, he was in grace. God took care of him, but after he sinned, he was then under the law, which got him put out the garden. Now, he had to take care of himself. Remember what we called this earlier? It's being separated from God.

Now, is there anything wrong with water baptism? No! However, the focus needs to be understood on why it's done.

Baptism is an open and public example of what happens to the soul when you are washed by the blood of Christ. It doesn't matter if you get baptized at a church, the park or the YMCA, because salvation isn't in the water. Salvation was received when you accepted Jesus.

Don't ever allow a man to tell you that the only way to salvation is through being dipped in the pool at the YMCA, because our justification isn't through water, it's through faith (Rom. 5:1).

"Spiritual Death Entered Into The World"
(3-B)

Being spiritually dead is to be separated from God (as we read earlier), but do we really understand what we are still connected to?

Although you may be spiritually dead, did you know that there is still a chance to be made alive?

Ephesians 2:5 says, *"Even when we were dead in sins, hath quickened us together with Christ, by grace ye are saved."*

So if salvation quickened us and made us alive, what happens to those who reject salvation?

Cords of Sin

When we were born, we were shaped in iniquity and conceived in sin (Psalms 51:5).

When we die, if we have not been born again, our sins will be as cords that will keep us attached to the death of our flesh.

Proverbs 5:22-23 says, *"His own iniquities shall take the wicked himself, and he shall be holden with the cords of his sins. He shall die without instruction; and in the greatness of his folly he shall go astray."*

It's just like when you were naturally born…when you came into this world you were attached to your mother at the navel. This is how sin has you connected, but when Christ enters, he cuts the cord and sets you free.

Don't kid yourself, there is nothing that a man can do to separate you from your sins.

Only the word is sharp enough, because it's sharper than any two-edged sword, piercing even to the dividing asunder of soul and spirit, joints and marrow and is even a discerner of the thoughts and intents of the heart (Hebrews 4:12).

If you reject Christ in this lifetime, a time will come when you will want him and he will not be available (John 8:21).

John 8:24 says, *"I said therefore unto you, that ye shall die in your sins: For if ye believe not that I am he, ye shall die in your sins."*

Jesus was very specific about the way

to be freed from the chords of sin. There is no grey. He clearly stated that if you do not believe that he is the Christ, you WILL die in your sins.

For those of us who do believe, we are placed in Christ and will no longer be subject to the law of sin and death.

Romans 8:1-2 says, *"There is therefore now no condemnation to them which are in Christ Jesus, who walk not after the flesh, but after the Spirit. For the law of the Spirit of life in Christ Jesus hath made me free from the law of sin and death."*

Faith Through Resurrection

Jesus came and paid a debt by dying as you and me. Through his sacrifice, we as Christians will never have to experience death, hell or the grave. Through his resurrection, our faith of eternal life was formed.

This is why we are crucified with Christ, because even though we are still in this body of flesh, we are not connected to it. This life that we live in the flesh, we can still live it by faith (Galatians 5:20).

So what does it really mean to be

crucified with Christ?

Well, it's when Jesus reconciled both himself and us together to God in one body, which came by the cross. So now, we have access to God and when he sees us, he'll see his son. He won't see our sins any longer.

The only way that we can still be in our sins after receiving salvation, is if Christ wasn't raised from the dead.

If he wasn't, then everybody who received Christ, both alive and dead, will never have the hope of being raised up. Our faith would be in vain (1 Cor. 15:12-22).

Can you imagine coming to church every Sunday, paying your tithes, dealing with church folk that you don't like and missing the football game, only to later find out that you're going to hell anyway? Why change your life around if the final outcome was going to be the same either way?

This is exactly why our faith is based on a God who rose from the dead, because now we have eternal life through him. We were given a hope of living beyond the death of our bodies, because we became translated from darkness to light.

Colossians 1:12-13 says, *"Giving thanks unto the Father, which hath made us meet to be partakers of the inheritance of the saints in light: Who hath delivered us from the power of darkness, and hath translated us into the kingdom of his dear son: In whom we have redemption through his blood, even the forgiveness of sins."*

New Conscience

When it came to the law, the only way to be delivered from sins were through sacrifices of goats and bulls (Heb. 10:1-5).

This happened year after year to remain pure from sin, but Jesus came as the lamb, so that his blood would sanctify us once and for all (Heb. 10:10).

If we have been sanctified once and for all, why do we remain to have a sin conscience? Why do we constantly ask God for forgiveness every time we make a mistake? Was our sins not covered under the blood?

God no longer remembers our sin, yet we continue to bring it up in prayer? Why is that? But so many churches teach people to come before God and confess your sins.

Look, once we are in Christ, there are no more sins to be forgiven of, because it was all forgiven on the cross, nearly two-thousand years ago!

If you still have a problem with sin, then you probably have a sinful nature, which means you need to come back to the altar and confess Christ for real. Once he's on the inside, your nature will change.

You won't want to do the same things you used to do. Why? Because your conscience (the Holy Spirit) will redirect you.

The places you used to go, the people you even used to hang-out with will all began to change.

It's important that we continue to deny the desires of our flesh, because if we don't, we'll be connected to it when our flesh dies.

Both the flesh and the spirit have a promised destination when you die. The flesh will return to the ground from where it came, and the spirit will return back to God (Ecclesiastes 12:7).

Only your soul has the freewill to choose its destiny…so who will you be connected to when your time is up?

Chapter 4:
Why Jesus Suffered Death For Every Man

Chapter 4:
"Why Jesus Suffered Death For Every Man"
(4-A)

So far we've learned about what Adam did, but we truly need to see what Christ did.

Receiving salvation may deliver us from the curse of Adam, but do we know what Christ had to go through, just for us to even enjoy the benefits of salvation?

Hebrews 2:9 says, *"But we see Jesus, who was made a little lower than the angels for the suffering of death, crowned with glory and honor; that he by the grace of God should taste death for every man."*

God made man a little lower than the angels, yet he became a man, so that through his death, man can be seated on high with him.

Once that happens, angels are subject to us. They are ministering spirits for us because we are heirs of salvation (Hebrews 1:14).

So why would he suffer death for us if he didn't have to? Why would he do such a thing in the first place? Well, all me to show you…

Why did Christ suffer death?

1) To Bring Many Sons Into Glory:
In the old covenant, you were slaves and servants, but in the new covenant we are made sons of God.

2) To Destroy The One Who Had The Power Of Death:
When Christ rose from the dead, he got up with all power in his hands. He destroyed the power of death and sin could no longer reign.

People today will preach to you that one day the devil is going to reign over the earth for a while, but how can that be true if he has no power?

The devil has already been defeated, so understand that Christ didn't die and give us power just to give it back to the devil.

3) To Be Our High Priest:
When he became our high priest, he knows how we feel. He has been through everything that we could ever go through,

because he was tempted as we were, but he didn't sin.

This is why we need to stop crying and complaining about how bad our situation is, causing us to talk as if Christ doesn't understand us.

He knows we aren't going to be perfect, but now that he is our high priest, we can come boldly to his throne and obtain both grace and mercy in our time of need (Hebrews 4:14-16).

4) *To Reconcile Us To Himself:*

He knew no sin, yet was made sin so we could become the righteousness of God in him. This is how we have become ambassadors for Christ (2 Cor. 5:18-21).

To be reconciled is to be in harmony. It's to fit like a glove, or to become one. This is what Christ has done with us, so we are now in harmony with him. We are as one with him, because we are now in him.

5) *To Become Poor So We Can Become Rich:*

The same God who has the whole world in his hands, became poor for our sake, so that through his poverty, we all could be made rich (2 Cor. 8:9).

Romans 8:32 says, *"He that spared not his own Son, but delivered him up for us all, how shall he not with him also freely give us all things?"*

He has given us all things that pertain to life and godliness (2 Peter 1:3), which are the riches for the natural and then also for the spiritual (Ephesians 1:3). If you find yourself poor in both, it may be time to revisit the altar!

If we can clearly see that he has given us everything, why are we still broke, busted and disgusted?

We only believe that we're poor, because we don't yet understand how rich we really are. So it's not a problem on God's end, it's the lack of our own knowledge that keeps us from knowing how to access it.

6) To Bring Us To God:

When we were in sin we were lost. Christ, who was just, suffered for the unjust, just so that we could find our way back to God. That's awesome all by itself!

1 Peter 3:18 says, *"For Christ also hath once suffered for sins, the just for the unjust, that he might bring us to God, being*

put to death in the flesh, but quickened by the Spirit."

7) *To Leave Us An Example:*

This last one is a hard one, because the church struggles with this without effort.

Christ came and left an example for us to follow after, but we can't say goodbye to our old habits and lifestyles.

1 Peter 2:21-24 says, *"For even hereunto were ye called: because Christ also suffered for us, leaving us an example, that ye should follow his steps: Who did no sin, neither was guile found in his mouth: who, when he was reviled, reviled not again; when he suffered, he threatened not; but committed himself to him that judgeth righteously."*

How many of us have messed that up already? He did no sin, so we have no excuse to act out from anger. He reviled not again, nor did he threaten anyone...yet we can't wait to shoot off at the mouth!

If we are going to be like Christ, we have to not play around and just do it. There is no alternative to righteous living, but death, hell and the grave. Why choose that if you don't have to?

Christ came to set an example for us to

follow after, so let's not take that lightly. If we live any kind of way, knowing that he suffered for us to live a completely different life, it's no different from spitting in his face.

Knowing this, do you still want to make excuses for your lifestyle?

"Why Jesus Suffered Death For Every Man"
(4-B)

Previously, we went over several reasons why Jesus suffered death for every man, but now we want to take it a step further.

Jesus suffered death so that we could all be saved by grace, but what does that really mean?

A few pages earlier, I showed you that if anything is done through grace, then it eliminates the effort of works. Nothing you can do can force grace, because grace is not the law.

In the old covenant, if you were to do something wrong, you were then guilty of breaking the whole law. Under grace, you don't have to do anything, because if you did, it would cease to be grace.

Ephesians 2:8 says, *"For by grace are ye saved through faith; and that not of yourselves: it is the gift of God: Not of works, lest any man should boast."*

Now, although we can see that

salvation was a gift, are you sure you understand exactly what had to happen for it to be that way?

God is spirit. Spirits cannot die. This is why he came and lived in a mortal body, so that he could suffer the same pain and anguish as we did. His sacrifice and death on the cross was for our sake.

It was through his death, burial and resurrection that we have been inherited with the grace to made righteous. So can you understand why it has nothing to do with anything you've done?

All that God asks us to do is to simply believe. That's it. If we keep his word, we shall never see death (John 8:51).

Fulfilling Righteousness

When Jesus was baptized by John, he did it to fulfill the law. Under the law, you had to be baptized. Jesus was still subject to all authority, so it was something he had to do.

Matthew 3:14-15 says, *"Then cometh Jesus from Galilee to Jordan unto John, to be baptized of him, But John forbad him, saying, I have need to be baptized of thee, and comest thou to me? And Jesus answered unto him, Suffer it to be so now: for thus it becometh us to fulfill all righteousness. "*

The more you read, you'll see Jesus mention the words, "Free", "Suffer", or "Suffering"…but what exactly does these things mean?

Passion/Suffering: *to feel what's painful to body and to the soul; grief and sorrow in the mind;*
Free: *to release from bondage, guilt, punishment, slavery and from self (the old man);*

For us to be made free from the law of sin and death, Jesus had to be made sin, so that the law might be fulfilled in us (Rom. 8:3-4).

Our freedom came at a price that we didn't have to pay, yet we still live in bondage?

The only way someone can still live in bondage after they have been set free, is if they don't know they're free…and the only way you can live and not know you're free, is if you never knew the truth.

John 8:32 says, *"And ye shall know the*

truth, and the truth shall make you free."

If you've followed the ministry of Paul, you'll see that his biggest enemy was the law. The message of grace was being preached, yet people still wanted to hold on to the law.

Did you know churches still do that today? They want you to come to Christ, but not if you're wearing jeans. They want you to receive salvation, as long as you do it through baptism.

They pretty much slap you with so many rules of tradition, all while not knowing that they're making the word of God of non-effect.

What does the way I dress have anything to do with my salvation? Isn't the church supposed to be the one place I can come to find God? Since when did he have rules on a dress code?

The church is saved by grace, yet we still operate under the law. You need to understand something, the law was given by Moses, but grace and truth came by Jesus Christ (John 1:17).

Once you are in Christ, you are free. There's nothing else you have to do. Now, we just need to realize we're free so we can live free.

Realizing You're Free

One thing that I've learned after being a pastor for many years, is that every Sunday I see the same people coming back to the altar for salvation, over and over and over again.

"Pastor, I messed up...I need salvation again, pastor!", or "Pastor, the Lord left me again. I had a beer and I don't wanna go to hell!"

Really? I wish I could tell them to just sit their butts down! God hasn't left you because of something you did. You were forgiven nearly two-thousand years ago!

The problem is this, most church folk are so sin-conscious that they feel a need to do things to keep God cool with them, but we've discussed this in a previous chapter, remember?

If you're born again, nothing can ever separate you from the love of God (Ro. 8:39), but we still need to die daily to our flesh.

Now, if you can't die to your flesh, then maybe your heart didn't truly allow

Christ on the inside. Are you mature enough to admit that?

Your sinful nature should change when Christ enters, but people treat Christ as a bungee-cord.

They strap him on at the altar so that they can jump back out into their old lifestyle, with the security of knowing he'll keep them from falling…God forbid!

We need to be smarter than this. Don't you understand that grace and peace is multiplied through the knowledge of God? Do we not have the mind of Christ?

As much grace as we need, we should be able to activate it at will, but it's not going to happen if we remain in ignorance.

Ignorance is darkness and darkness is as sin. That's why the best way to be free is to just die…for he that is dead is freed from sin (Ro. 6:7).

When it's all said and done, either you will be dead "in" your sins, or you will be dead "to" your sins. There is no middle ground. You will either die to the flesh, or die in it.

1 Peter 4:1-2 says, *"Forasmuch then as Christ hath suffered for us in the flesh, arm yourselves likewise with the same mind:*

for he that hath suffered in the flesh hath ceased from sin; That he no longer should live the rest of his time in the flesh to the lusts of men, but to the will of God."

Chapter 5:
Fear Entered Into The World

Chapter 5
"Fear Entered Into The World"
(5-A)

When we go back to when Adam first sinned, we'll see that not only did sin and death enter the world, but fear did as well.

Genesis 3:9-10 says, *"And the Lord God called unto Adam, and said unto him, Where art thou? And he said, I heard thy voice in the garden, and I was afraid, because I was naked; and I hid myself."*

Now, we can clearly see that sin had taken effect, because his fear caused him to lie.

Adam said that he was afraid because he was naked, but we know he was born naked and lived without shame (Genesis 2:25). So what can cause a man to hide from the presence of God? Fear!

Well, what exactly is fear? When the bible mentions the word "fear", it's not referring to the fear of heights or spiders, so you can squash that mentality. Here's a definition for you...

Fear: *the effect or consequence of guilt/or a condemned conscience; an evil expectation; the lack of courage and faith; the spirit of defeat; the spirit of bondage*

As you can see, Adam had a condemned conscience. He hid when God called him. Many of us don't realize it, but we do the exact same thing.

How many times have you just walked around in defeat? Maybe you know someone who does? To accept defeat is to accept the fact that you cannot overcome. If you cannot overcome, then you are no more than a slave in bondage.

Fear is the spirit of the devil, not God. Instead, God gave us the spirit of power, love and a sound mind (2 Tim. 1:7).

When you are still in Adam, you'll have the spirit of fear, but when you are born again, God gives you power to rule. You'll have the power to say no to your carnal mind, so that you can now mortify the deeds of your flesh.

Well, what happens if I accept Christ, but I still have a problem or an addiction that I can't shake, does this mean I'm not reigning with power and dominion?

If you are a born-again believer, but you cannot rule over your flesh, it's only evident that you aren't ruling because you are still in bondage.

The Spirit of Bondage

To be in bondage, is to be in slavery. When you are in sin, you are a slave to sin. People that are in bondage have no power, because if they did, would they remain in bondage?

Due to the fact that we are all born into sin through Adam, we have inherited the spirit of fear, along with sin and death. Salvation is like being adopted, because we are now part of a new family.

Romans 8:14-15 says, *"For as many as are led by the Spirit of God, they are the sons of God. For ye have not received the spirit of bondage again to fear; but ye have received the Spirit of adoption, whereby we cry, Abba, Father."*

Once you are placed in Christ, you are then made a son. Not a slave. You can only be a slave when you are operating under the law. A slave cannot abide in the house of a master, only a son can.

This is deep, because you can't be both a son and a slave. If you can't control yourself when it comes to sin, then you are a slave of sin.

John 8:34-36 says, *"Jesus answered them, Verily, verily, I say unto you, Whosoever committeth sin is the servant of sin. And the servant abideth not in the house for ever: but the Son abideth ever. If the Son therefore shall make you free, ye shall be free indeed."*

So, how are we made free? To be made free is to be created free, just as Adam was made in the garden. He was created. We must now be created free as new creatures in Christ.   What are we actually being freed from? We are being made free from the curse of Adam!

We are free from the laws of sin, death and from the chords of sin that will try to keep us tied to our flesh when it dies.

Christ was our deliverer, but I'm going to show you that not only was Adam type and shadow of Christ, but so was Moses.

A Quick Comparison

Moses was type and shadow of Christ,

because he was placed in Egypt (which represents the world) to free his people who were enslaved to bondage. However, Moses delivered them from a natural Pharaoh, Christ actions were spiritual.

Moses was a Hebrew, but was later adopted by Egyptians. God came down to live in the flesh, so that he could be as us. He who knew no sin, became sin for us.

No matter how far down into the story you get, you'll still see the comparison to Christ through Moses. Just keep this in mind, Moses was under the law. Christ is under grace.

Under the law, you had to continue in God's word, because the Holy Spirit had not yet come. Under grace, all you have to do is abide in him and his word will abide in you.

Although God used Moses to lead Israel out of Egypt, they still ended up in the wilderness for forty years. They knew who God was, but they didn't "know" God. If they did, they would not have made any graven images (Gen. 32:1-10).

To truly be set free, you have to know the truth. To "know" is used intimately here.

You can't just know the truth through water baptism, you have to develop a real relationship with Christ. The word must come into you and birth new life.

You can't just come to church, hear the word, feel good and go home like nothing ever happened. Knowing the truth is not a one-night stand.

Dealing with Fear

When it comes to being free, our faith is very important and it plays a huge role. If we don't believe we are free, we'll revert back to the "old us" and find ourselves being slaves to sin again. Slaves cannot be overcomers.

1 John 5:4 says, *"For whatsoever is born of God overcometh the world: and this is the victory that overcometh the world, even our faith."*

So what does that scripture mean when it refers to "whatsoever"? It's talking about your soul.

When your soul is born of God, you can overcome the world, which we learned earlier in chapter 1-A, is your flesh.

When we are in Christ we have nothing to worry about, because he promised us peace during times of tribulation. There's nothing we have to do but to remain in Christ, because he has already overcame the world (John 16:33).

People make this fact so complicated, because they still feel the need to "make something happen". Why attempt to overcome a situation that Christ has already overcome?

Since we are in him, we can enjoy the benefits of being victorious. All we have to do is use our faith and believe it's done.

2 Corinthians 4:13 says, *"We having the same spirit of faith, according as it is written, I believed, and therefore have I spoken; we also believe, and therefore speak."*

What is it that you speak? Do you constantly speak of victory and how great things are in your life, or are you always speaking about how messed up your world is?

Remember, we learned earlier that we eat from our own bellies. If we speak it, we can bring it to pass. This is one of the benefits of being a victorious believer in Christ…so why use that power to curse yourself?

If you never learn to control your

flesh, the enemy will find a way in and cause you lose and waste your power. It's what he's wanted since the beginning. He just needed someone foolish enough to give it away.

It's like the story of Jacob and Esau (Exodus 27). Jacob was the younger brother, so Esau had inherited the birthright. He was promised to have everything his father had, but he didn't realize what it was worth.

Due to his nature of being in the fields, he never understood the true value of his own inheritance. So when he grew hungry, he sold his birthright to his little brother for a bowl of soup.

Being in the flesh makes it hard for you to obtain the things of God. It's like you're already dead to God, but once you come to Christ, you're made alive, so why would you want to still be like the dead?

Do you think you have an Esau syndrome? Are you willing to trade away your heavenly inheritance for a bowl of ramen noodles?

Romans 8:9-10 says, *"So they that are in the flesh cannot please God. But ye are not in the flesh, but in the Spirit, if so be that the Spirit of God dwell in you. Now if any man have not the Spirit of Christ, he is none of his. And if Christ be in you, the body is dead because of sin; but the Spirit is life because of righteousness. "*

"Fear Entered Into The World"
(5-B)

One of the greatest forces that needs to be destroyed in the church is ignorance. There are so many people out here that don't know the bible, but as soon as someone teaches the truth, they turn away…but ignorance will be destroyed before you get to the end of this book!

In order to really get deeper into the truth of Adam, we need to dig deeper into his genealogy. So allow me to take the time to explain the genealogy of both Adam and Christ…

Adam & Christ: The Genealogy

In the bible there are two Adams. The first Adam was natural, the new covenant Adam (Jesus) is spirit (I Cor. 15:47).

The first Adam was natural because he was made with hands, but Christ was conceived by the Holy Spirit (Matt. 1:20).

I Corinthians 15:44-45 says, *"It is sown a natural body; it is raised a spiritual body. There is a natural body, and there is a spiritual body. And is it is written, The first man Adam was made a living soul; the last Adam was made a quickening spirit."*

Can you see the two men? Adam was made from the earth, Christ was not. Both had a purpose and a legacy that was left behind. Let's look at the genealogy of Christ first…

Matthew 1:1 says, *"The Book of the generation of Jesus Christ, the son of David, the son of Abraham."*

Christ was born to be king, because he was the heir of David. Being the son of Abraham gives him all the blessings that were promised to Abraham. Can you see how he was destined to have everything?

Even Mary and Joseph had a purpose. Parenting Jesus was no accident. We know Mary was chosen because she was pure, but the bible traces Joseph's bloodline from his father, all the way back to Adam, which was also the son of God (Luke 3:23-38). Isn't that amazing?

If you read Luke 3:23-38, you'll see a few names within that timeline that we will touch on in a moment. Names like, Seth, Enos and Mathusala…any of those sound familiar? If not, don't worry. We'll come back to them.

How much do you really know about Adam? Did you know Man was created to be made a little lower than the angels?

Adam was made to have dominion over the works of his hands and all things under his feet (Ps. 8:4-9). But when he ate of the tree, he lost his dominion, causing so much fear to enter his heart that he couldn't even be in the presence of God.

Here is something you need to understand before we continue…God did not start the bible off with man as "nations", but if you have the revelation of it, then you can see that he did. What does this mean? Allow me to explain…

Day One: God created the heaven and the earth. He created light and divided the light from darkness (Gen. 1:1-5).

Day Two: God created a firmament in the midst of the waters to divide the waters from the waters. He divided the waters below the firmament and the waters above and called the firmament heaven (Gen. 1:6-8).

Day Three: God called the dry land Earth and named the waters "the seas". He caused the earth to bring forth grass and fruit whose seed was in itself (Gen. 1:9-13).

Day Four: God created the two lights, one to rule the day and the other one to rule the night. We know these now as the sun and the moon (Gen. 1:14-19).

Day Five: God created the fowls of the air and the fish of the sea, both small and great. He then blessed them, telling them to be fruitful and multiply (Gen. 1:20-23).

Day Six: God created the beasts of the field and then created man and woman in his likeness. He gave "them" dominion over the beasts of the field, the fowls of the air and the fish in the sea (Gen. 1:24-31).

Day Seven: When God seen that everything that he created was good, he rested. He then blessed the seventh day and even sanctified it (Gen. 2:1-3).

Can you see how everything was put together? What you just read was the "Generations of the Heavens and the Earth"

(Gen. 2:4). The creation of life cannot be disputed.

Everything that was made by God was good, but there was a small issue…it had never rained and there was no one to till the ground (Gen. 2:5). Can you now see the reason for creating Adam in Genesis 2:7?

Man and female were created on day six, yet there was no one to till the ground? How did they lose their authority and dominion? Who took it from them?

Something tragic had to happen for God to create Adam, which makes all of this so interesting, because we see that Christ had the same mission when he came.

When God started the book of Matthew, he started out with the generations of Jesus Christ. When he started the book of Genesis, he started the generations of Heaven and Earth (Gen. 2:4), and then with the generations of Adam (Gen. 5:12).

What is the correlation between Christ and Adam? They were both sons of God. Remember what we read in Luke 3?

The original mission for Christ when he came was to save the world (Jn. 3:17), the same can be said of Adam, who was created to keep an unkept garden.

Sin was already here when Christ came, just as it was there when Adam was created. Both were equipped to rule and have dominion, but the first Adam failed. So when Christ came, he took back the dominion and power that the devil stole from Adam then gave that same power to those who believed on his name (Jn. 1:12).

Can't you see how important you are to God? He sent his own son to correct Adam's mistake, so that you and I can operate in the same power and dominion that we were created to have.

Thanks to Christ, we now have the power to be sons of God, because we are now in Christ who has risen from the dead with all power in his hands. We are in him and he is in us. So do you still think you're just human?

If you are not in Christ, you are still in your sins. It's like you are still dead to God until you are made alive. So why does a good faith-teaching church play such a crucial role in our lives?

Well, if we see it as it was in the time of Noah, we'd see how all that were not in the ark had died, but Christ is not type and shadow of the ark, he's type and shadow of

Noah. The ark is representation of the church.

Noah built the ark, just as Christ built the church. In that day, only Noah was righteous and it takes a righteous man to build a church. All those who believed went in, but those who didn't had perished.

The Good & Evil Generations

When we look at the generations of Adam, we'll see that they started from his two sons, Cain and Able. Cain represents the evil seed, Able represents the other.

Now, if you don't believe that others were here before Adam was created, then you will only have Adam and Cain remaining, because Able was killed by Cain. So who is Seth?

Able was the righteous seed, but when Cain killed him (Gen. 4:8), God later raised up Seth. Through Seth (Enos), the righteous generation could continue to call upon the name of the Lord (Gen. 4:25-26). Able represents the old man, Seth represents the resurrected man.

As punishment for his sin, the Lord cursed Cain. He said that anyone who kills him, vengeance will be taken upon them sevenfold (Gen. 4:11-15).

Wait, I thought no one was here but Adam, Eve and Cain? Who is the "Anyone" that the Lord talked about? How can vengeance be taken out on "them" if no one was here but his mother and father?

Remember what happened on the sixth day? This is where "they" came from. "They" were created to have dominion, but lost it…which is why Adam was later created.

Still having doubts? Try this…After Cain was cursed and driven out of the presence of the Lord, he went east of Eden to the land of Nod. There, he found a wife and bare a son named Enoch (Gen. 4:16-17).

Okay, how did Cain find a wife if no one was here but he and his parents? So his wife was already here? How can we explain her existence unless we admit that there were people here before the creation of Adam?

To deny that, you'd have to blatantly deny the validity of the bible, scriptures and all. We have to get to a point where we believe what the bible say, not what men say.

Cain didn't leave the presence of his family and go marry his sister, because

Adam and Eve didn't have daughters until years after Seth was born. So this eliminates the theory of Cain running off with his sister, because he "found" a wife, not grew up with her.

Man may have good intentions, but when they don't know the word, they end up contaminating minds…mine included, but I thank the Lord for removing ignorance from my life.

Can you see how the truth has been in the bible all of this time, yet we only read the surface? What a huge mistake on our part!

God sent his son to save. He did it with the first Adam, he also did again with the second Adam. One was natural, the other was spiritual.

When we look back at Cain after he found a wife and had a son, several generations passed down before Adam and Eve gave birth to Seth (Gen. 4:17-25).

The evil seed had spread. Men didn't call upon the name of the Lord anymore. This is exactly why Seth was born.

Can you see his purpose now? Every move that God made had a specific purpose. Always remember that.

The same can be said of Noah. In his

time, the wickedness of man was great in the earth and the Lord was willing to destroy mankind, but Noah found grace in the eyes of the Lord (Gen. 6:5-8).

Noah's purpose was to build an ark, because God saw that the earth was corrupt with sin and violence.

The daughters of Cain (man/flesh) married the Sons of Seth (God/righteous), and this angered the Lord (Gen. 6:1-2).The righteous is not to go out and marry the wicked.

Do you think God was going to destroy the righteous? No! He was going to destroy the wicked and spare the righteous, but only Noah and his small family were the only righteous people left.

Wow, that's all? Clearly we can see that only ignorance can blind the eyes of the creation to the creator. Have your eyes been blinded?

"Fear Entered Into The World"
(5-C)

The more that we understand Adam's failure, the more we can appreciate what Christ did.

In the old days, sacrifices were needed to cleanse sins. They used the blood of lambs and goats, but when Jesus came, he became the ultimate sacrifice. His blood washed all of our sins away.

So why is the blood so important? It's because the life of the flesh is in the blood (Lev. 17:11). Without the blood, there can be no forgiveness.

Hebrews 9:22 says, *"And almost all things are by the law purged with blood; and without shedding of blood is no remission."*

When we are naturally born, we are born into sin (or into Adam). We have the old nature and a sinful conscience. Remember what happened in the days of Noah? It angered God to see such wickedness in man.

God destroyed man, leaving only Noah and his family to replenish the earth (Gen. 9:1) then promised to never destroy man or the earth by water again (Gen. 9:11).

Man was given a chance to plead his case and have forgiveness through the offering of burnt sacrifices and blood. This became a ritual that only the high priest (the righteous man) could perform for himself and the people (Heb. 9:6-10).

So when Christ came, he became our high priest. No longer did we need the blood of goats and calves, because by his own blood he redeemed us (Heb. 9:11-12)

Hebrews 9:14-15 says, *"How much more shall the blood of Christ, who through the eternal Spirit offered himself without spot to God, purge your conscience from dead works to serve the living God? And for this cause he is the mediator of the new testament, that by means of death, for the redemption of the transgressions that were under the first testament, they which are called might receive the promise of eternal inheritance."*

Did you understand what that scripture means? Christ became our offering for sin. Although we were under the transgressions of Adam (the first testament), Christ became our mediator so that we may receive an eternal inheritance.

Isn't that awesome? All we have to do is believe on what took place nearly two-thousand years ago on the cross. It's that simple!

When you aren't saved, you are still a part of Adam, which is considered the "corruptible seed". However, when you believe on the death, burial and resurrection of Christ, you are then born of God, which is the "incorruptible" (I Pet. 1:23).

Understanding the Law/Guilt

There is a difference between being guilty and having guilt. When you have guilt, you are judged according to the facts. It doesn't matter how you feel. However, when you're guilty, you feel as if your actions will be condemned.

Guilt: *the facts, not the feeling of committing wrong.*
Guilty: *the effect of the conscience of guilt; to be held accountable*

When it comes to the law, you need to understand who it applied to. The law was given to God's people (Israel) by Moses to govern them so that they had a standard for righteous living.

Christ's death caused him to fulfill the law, allowing all those who came after him to reside in grace. All we have to do for that grace is simply accept it and receive it.

We were never under the law. The Jews were. It was they who kept the law until Christ came.

Keep this in mind...to continue to keep the law after Christ had already fulfilled it, it then becomes self-righteousness. This is the issue that the Apostle Paul had with the Jews.

So why are we always so guilt-conscience? It's because of this old man, Adam. Let's look at it this way...

In your mind, draw a horizontal straight line. Everything under that line will represent Adam and the law. Everything above that line will represent Christ and grace.

When you are born and come to an age to know the difference between what's right and wrong, you are underneath that line. You are considered a "corruptible seed", you **will** be judged and you **will** die in your sins.

It is here where you are considered

guilty before God and you cannot be justified in his sight (Rom. 3:19-20).

When you believe on Christ, you are then translated from the bottom of that line onto the top of it (Col. 1:13). You are now considered an "incorruptible seed".

It is here where you have eternal life, along with everything else Christ left for you after the cross.

Judgment only takes place below that line, because once you are above that line, there is no more condemnation (Rom. 8:1).

The problem is this, most Christians who are translated onto the top of that line still continue to think like the ones underneath it.

This is why you must continue to renew your mind and change the way you think. You are the righteousness of God, not an old wretched sinner.

Good Credit

When it comes to being guilty, there must be a judge. Only God can judge, so do not judge each other (Rom. 14:13).

Remember that line we made a second ago? When you are above that line, you can't be judged anyway.

For you to even be considered guilty, you must have an account. It's almost like a police record. After your name is in the system, everything you've done wrong is listed under your account.

As Christians, it's not possible to play the fence here. Either you are saved or you're not. You can't stand before the judgment seat and the throne of grace at the same time, because there's no condemnation under grace.

Some preachers will tell you that although you won't go to hell, you'll only be judged according to your works. Oh, Really?

Look, to be judged is to be judged. There's no grey area. Since we are in grace, we don't have to be sin conscience, because Christ paid our debt.

The only issue now is that we fail to realize it, and because we fail to understand that, we automatically think we're going to be judged for our mistakes, but that's not true.

Look at it this way…do you pay a bill for a credit card that you don't own?

Think about it, if you got a bill in the mail that stated you had three brand new

Bentleys and all three payments were due, what you do? I'm sure you'd freak out, especially if you were living in your parents basement, waiting on your unemployment check to come.

These examples may be a bit crazy, but hopefully you're getting a better understanding of your "account".

For a person to have an account, "works" must be present. Works represent what "you" have done, which makes it self-righteousness.

Abraham was well-known for his faith. It wasn't through his works that justified him, because he chose to completely believe God. By doing so, it was counted to him as righteousness (Rom. 4:1-5).

If Abraham was justified by believing God, how are you then justified? By believing! When you believe God, it is counted on your account as righteousness.

If you went into a store and had a gift-card, but you weren't sure how much you had on it, how would you shop? Would you shop scared and cheap?

Well, let's say that the store clerk ran your card and told you that you had a credit balance of one-million dollars, how different would your shopping attitude be then?

This is how grace works, because no matter how many times we mess up, we can't use up enough grace in a lifetime. His grace is sufficient for us (2 Cor. 12:9).

We have an account with God that can never be overdrawn, so now can you see how you sound when you go before God after making a mistake? It's already been debited!

Grace is the best thing to happen to man since deodorant, so never feel that it will perspire or run out. It's yours as long as you remain on the topside of that horizontal line you just drew.

When you hear someone tell you that you are going to be judged, you can look at them and laugh, but only if you are born again.

When you are born again, your flesh was judged and sin was removed. You can't be judged again. How could you? Can you be charged, convicted and judged of a crime that happened in Minnesota on the same day you were on a cruise to Jamaica?

You can't be a suspect if you have no ties to the case. This is what it means to be free from the cords of sin, because once those ties are cut, there is nothing connecting you to be found guilty.

Now, we no longer need to remain with a guilty conscience, because when God sees our record, he only sees the blood of his son and considers us innocent…case dismissed!

Chapter 6:
The Curse Entered Into The World

Chapter 6:
"The Curse Entered Into The World"
(6-A)

When Adam sinned, there were a chain of events that took place. So far we've read how sin, fear and death all entered into the world, but now we are going to look at another one…the curse.

To fully grasp the depth of the curse, we need to understand what it is and what it represents when concerning the heart of man. So here are a few definitions…

Curse: *condemnation (judgment); to corrupt; to make powerless; bound; the disfavor of God; doomed for punishment;*

Due to the disobedience of Adam, the ground was cursed, which we learned earlier was the heart. Thorns and thistles arose from the ground, causing them to eat from the herb of the field (Gen. 3:17-19).

The bible does an excellent job on how it represents types and shadows, but if you look at the example of Christ, you'll see how important his death on the cross was.

Jesus had a conversation with Pilate about how his kingdom was not of this world (Jn. 18:36-37), but the Jews didn't even acknowledge him as their king (Jn. 19:12-15).

So out of mockery, when Jesus was being crucified, he was given a crown of thorns to wear on his head (Matt. 27:29). The crown of thorns is representation of man's curse that was placed upon his head.

Everything that Jesus did on earth had a purpose. Keep that in mind, because I'm going to show you a lot more as we go deeper into this chapter.

A New Leaf?

The bible is spirit, yet people without revelation will try to understand it in the natural. You can't use your earthly logic to understand the things of God.

I once had a woman who asked me a question about the Garden of Eden. She asked me if the trees in the garden were actual trees or did they represent something else...so I gave her the same information I gave to you, but can you remember what you've learned? Let's do a quick recap...

Earlier I showed you what the world was, remember? The world is your flesh. You are to love not the things of world, nor anything in it (1 Jn. 2:15-17), because there is no good thing in the flesh (Rom. 7:18).

Your heart is a garden, which is why you must be careful of what you allow to take root in it...because if you are unsaved, your heart is an unkept garden, which we know as the field (we're coming back to this).

We are the seeds, trees that will either produce good fruit or corrupt fruit. The righteous seeds shall prosper, but the tares (ungodly) will be driven away (Ps. 1:3-4).

Since Adam sinned, the curse made it impossible for the ground to yield fruit. Now, he was forced to sweat and work for his own food, rather than relaxing in the shade while God supplied his needs.

If you can see this spiritually, you can see how this affects the unbeliever.

Have you ever known someone who doesn't practice what they preach? What you are witnessing is how their actions are speaking louder than their words.

Your actions and the result of your actions are your fruit. A good tree can't bare bad fruit, just as a bad tree cannot produce good fruit (Matt. 7:16-20).

So how is it that you can turn over a new leaf every year? If the tree has corrupt fruit, the leaves won't mean a hill of beans, regardless of how pretty they are.

If you wouldn't buy a Corvette without an engine, you definitely wouldn't eat rotten fruit from a pretty tree. It's the same concept.

When you are unsaved, it doesn't matter how much work you put into being a good person, you can never receive eternal life and salvation that way. Your works are self-righteous and can never yield fruit.

Salvation is a free gift that we don't have to work for, just as being born into sin wasn't something we had control over. One man got us into sin and one man got us out.

Can you see a better comparison between Adam and Christ now? They both had a main focus and an objective.

Adam's job was to till the ground (heart) and keep it, but he failed. So Christ was then sent to save the heart, because it was lost.

A Cursed Nature?

Once you are born again, you are no longer bound by sin. But what exactly is the sin that had you bound? Well, it wasn't anything that you did.

We tend to think that we are in sin when we make mistakes, such as sex, drinking, cursing, etc…but these things are not what got us into sin. There is only one sin that caused us to be in sin, which was Adam's disobedience to God.

Will we make mistakes? Absolutely! However, you must understand that we are saved by grace.

Remember the example I used earlier with the unlimited gift card? No matter what we do, we can never be sinners again.

We are in Christ now and there is no sin in Christ. Those who are not in Christ are still bound by the sin of Adam. This is why their nature is still "disobedience".

When a person is unsaved, they can't obey. You can tell them and even show them how to live right, but they can't do it. If they can, it won't be for long because their nature won't allow them to maintain it. Let's look at it from a godly perspective.

If you are in Christ, there are some things that you know you don't desire to do. You may be dead to drugs, but regardless of how good someone else makes it sound, you don't want it. It's not in your nature.

Can you teach a dog to cut his own hair, or maybe even to speak proper English? It's natural that people will automatically think you're crazy, because everyone knows that it's not in the dog's nature to do those things. All he will do is whine and bark.

The nature of sin and the nature of righteousness are two completely different things. This is why believers aren't supposed to marry unbelievers, just as the sons of Seth married the daughters of Cain (Gen. 6:1-7).

If you claim to be born again, yet your nature is to openly abuse the grace of God, then you may need to reconsider your salvation. You can't say that you are a Christian and then live your life any kind of way.

When we make mistakes, it's good to know that we have already been forgiven, but the fruit of our true nature is revealed when we continue to walk after the flesh, especially after claiming we're dead to sin.

"What shall we say then? Shall we

continue in sin, that grace may abound? God
forbid. How shall we, that are dead to sin,
live any longer therein?" – Romans 6:1-2

Chapter 6:
"The Curse Entered Into The World"
(6-B)

As we continue to understand how the curse entered into the world, we see that the root of it came through disobedience.

God gave Adam the complete freedom to eat of every tree in the garden, but he also gave him the direct command to completely stay away from the tree of the knowledge of good and evil (Gen. 2:15-17).

Eve also had the complete freedom to do the same, but after being tempted of the devil, she saw and desired the forbidden tree, later causing her husband to partake with her (Gen. 3:6).

Once Eve ate of the tree, her heart became cursed. Adam partook of it, causing his heart to become cursed as well. So keep this in mind, if the ground (the heart) is cursed, the fruit will also be cursed.

Can you now see why Christ came as the tree of life? He came to restore what was once cursed.

For us to be fruitful would be a beautiful thing, but what if we haven't accepted the tree of life? Everything we do and touch will be corrupt, just like a bad apple once you mix it in with the other fresh apples.

Earlier in this book, we went over the three curses that are in a man's heart when he isn't born again…do you remember what they were? Let's visit 1 John 2:15-17.

1) *The Lust of the Flesh*
2) *The Lust of the Eyes*
3) *The Pride of Life*

Now, although these three are born into us through Adam, we are given the power to cut these ties when we are born again through Christ. However, if we do not abide under the grace that was given to us through Christ, we are then subject to the law.

In the law, there were twelve curses that were written in Deuteronomy 27. The law was created to give man a standard for righteous living before Christ came, but breaking these laws would cause a curse to come into your life.

We should be beyond thankful that Christ came and fulfilled the law, because I doubt we would've been able to keep the law.

If you don't think I'm serious, read the following (Deut. 27:15-26) to see which one would've had you stoned:

- *Cursed be the man that makes idols*
- *Cursed be he that setteth light by his father or his mother.*
- *Cursed be he that removes his neighbor's landmark.*
- *Cursed be he that makes the blind to wander out of the way.*
- *Cursed be he that perverts the judgment of the stranger, fatherless, and widow.*
- *Cursed be he that sleeps with his father's wife.*
- *Cursed be he that sleeps with any manner of beast.*
- *Cursed be he that sleeps with his sister.*
- *Cursed be he that sleeps with his mother-in-law.*
- *Cursed be he that killeth his neighbor in secret.*
- *Cursed be he that takes a reward to slay the innocent.*
- *Cursed be he that confirms not all of the words of this law to do them.*

Can you see how easily we would've

been stoned?

You may not have been guilty of sleeping with animals, but maybe you prefer to stay home on Sunday and wash your new car?

Maybe you prefer to spend more time with your girlfriend rather than spending time in prayer? Regardless, that's considered idol worship. Why? Because anything you place before God is an idol.

Maybe idol worship isn't your thing, but I'm sure you may have cut your grass one day and eased on over and took a few feet off your neighbor's yard to make your lawn look bigger…we've all done it, but thank God we won't be stoned for it.

The law was intended for Israel to rely on their works and righteousness, to prove to God that they were his. Now, we no longer need to "do" anything. All we have to do is receive it.

"But that no man is justified by the law in the sight of God, it is evident: for, The just shall live by faith. And the law is not of faith: but, The man that doeth them shall live in them. Christ hath redeemed us from the curse of the law, being made a curse for us: for it is written, Cursed is every one that hangeth on

a tree: That the blessings of Abraham might come on the Gentiles through Jesus Christ; that we might receive the promise of the Spirit through faith." – Galatians 3:11-14

Isn't that amazing? Where would we be right now if grace had not yet come? We should be completely grateful that sin is no longer our master, because we are no longer under the law (Rom. 6:14).

Philosophy & Vain Deceit

Now that we are under grace, we must be careful at all times of what we allow in our hearts. Whatever we sow or allow to be sown in our hearts will reap either good fruit or corruption.

What does this mean? It means that there are some ministers and some churches you need to stay away from. Many people still preach the law and not grace, which only leads to a church full of scared and corrupt members.

Here's a brief definition of the word "corrupt" that I want to explain a bit further.

Corrupt: *defiled; unholy/unclean; spoiled; rotten*

The purpose of going to church isn't just to shout, dance, feel good and go home. In fact, if you don't receive the word and meditate on it afterwards, you're going to church for nothing.

Why go to a church when you aren't seeing a change in your life? If you aren't really learning anything, can you really blame the minister, or do you blame yourself for sticking around?

When we allow ourselves to sit under a ministry that teaches law, we hinder our own growth. Didn't we just read how we aren't justified through the law? So why continue to waste our Sundays?

Ministers that teach the law will tell you what you can and can't do. It forces you to almost live in fear of going to hell, but that's not what the ministry of grace is all about.

The reason we continue to sit under these types of churches, is because they have a great choir, or the pastor "sure can preach"...but what does the word say about such churches?

"Beware lest any man spoil you through philosophy and vain deceit, after the

tradition of men, after the rudiments of the world, and not after Christ." – Colossians 2:8

The word of God is powerful, but if it is preached incorrectly, it becomes ineffective.

Why do you think so many church members are Christians but have no power? Why do you think people are going to church every Sunday but never change?

When you are serious about the word, you can't sit under a ministry where only one scripture is read, the rest is spent by screaming before you're sent home...you can't settle for that!

What's really sad is that people will fight you when you tinker with their religion. It's a clear indication on how you know they have been receiving vain doctrine.

People may not realize it, but when you sit in a church where they won't let a woman visit because she's wearing pants, there's a problem and you better find your way out fast!

When a person upholds the teaching of the church rather than the teachings of the word, they become a dangerous force to new believers. Why is that?

It's because they refuse to read the bible for themselves, so the preaching that they receive becomes a security blanket that they can't let go of, causing them to reject everything else...even the truth.

Do you know anyone like that? Do you know of anyone that will fight you if you explain to them the truth about an issue? It's crazy because you know they haven't studied the word for themselves, but they will surely fight you over what their pastor told them.

We need to get away from some of our spiritual bad habits, plain and simple. We can't just accept council based off of what people think. It has to be what God says.

When Adam harkened to Eve, she had already been corrupted. The moment he believed her, his heart became corrupted as well. Who's harkening to you?

Can you see now why it's so important to have your heart and your mind renewed?

We must learn to watch what we say, because it will come to pass. Our tongue is for blessings, not to curse.

This is why God designed a prison for the tongue...he gave you teeth (built-in bars), lips (built-in curtain), just to keep your tongue locked and in check. It's not what goes into a man, but what comes of his heart that defiles him (Matt. 15:16-20).

Chapter 6:
"The Curse Entered Into The World"
(6-C)

"Be not deceived; God is not mocked: for whatsoever a man soweth, that shall he also reap. For he that soweth to his flesh shall of the flesh reap corruption; but he that soweth to the Spirit shall of the Spirit reap life everlasting" – Galatians 6:7-8

Galatians 6:7-8 isn't referring to your finances. In fact, the word "sow" in this verse isn't about giving money at all. It's actually referring to "living", because when you are put into Christ, you are "sown" into Christ.

This is why if you live your life in the flesh you will live a life of corruption, because if you leave your soul in the flesh, it will corrupt. Allow me to explain…

Your soul is who you are. It's your immortal form that's trapped in a mortal and corrupt shell. If you die as is (unsaved), your soul will forever be attached to the cords of your decaying flesh. However, if you are born again through Christ, those cords to your soul are now cut, allowing your soul to enter the presence of the Lord.

The best way to visualize this is by seeing your flesh standing in a grave, stretching out and attaching his hand to your soul, which is floating in mid-air. Your spirit has your other hand, while standing halfway into heaven.

Your soul is caught between the two, but if you're born of God, your flesh has no hold on you. This is why you must sow to your spirit, because he needs to be strong enough to yank your soul away from the corruption of sin.

But how sad is it when you realize that you willingly rejected the word of God, which was the only possible sword sharp enough to make you free?

Can you now easily understand why Jesus came? He came to set your soul free from the bonds of sin, not to take your money. Only the thief comes to steal, kill and destroy…but who is the thief?

We all want to say it's the devil, but the devil has no power. He can only be effective if we give him place, just like Eve did in the beginning. Our thief is a lot more personal, because it's the lust of our eyes, the lust of our flesh and the pride of life.

Having these three in your heart will only guarantee that they will cause corruption, because there is no good thing in the flesh.

These things were born into our very DNA, but being born into Christ will remove them permanently.

When you don't want the word, you are giving place to the devil, which is only an open invitation for him to have control over your life. All he's going to do is drive your life right into the ground. What, did you think he was going to come in and be responsible?

The only way to evict the devil for good is by allowing Christ to come in on the inside and live.

We can actually rejoice, because being born of Christ places us under grace which provides us with unlimited favor. We don't even have to resist the devil anymore, because the grace over our lives will keep the devil away.

If our lives are constantly under attack by the enemy, then it's only proof that we are still walking after the flesh which is really the old nature. How can the enemy affect your life if Christ is on the inside? Is Christ really that weak, or is he just purely absent?

You can't lie to yourself. If you are still living your life your way, you're still walking after the flesh. If you put on the old nature just to have a fun weekend, can you blame God when things "accidentally" go wrong?

If you remained under his protection and guidance, you wouldn't even have those type of problems. God doesn't make mistakes. We do.

Baptized into The Body of Love

When you read Romans 6, you'll see how our old nature is crucified with Christ, destroying the sin in our bodies.

Romans 6:7 reads, "For he that is dead is freed from sin."

Once you are crucified with Christ, you are then risen with him. When you are risen with him, you should now be like him. This means we need to love one another, but this can't be done when we are still living for ourselves.

When you aren't born again, you can't love. It's not in your nature to love. In fact, you're selfish with who you love, because you still think this life is all about you and how you live it up. Well, you're absolutely wrong!

It's always easy to love those that love you back, but what about those people you don't like at all? They may hate you with a passion, but it's our job to still love them anyway.

I know you may be shaking your head in disagreement, because why stress over loving people who you feel may be irrelevant? Well, God loved you, didn't he?

That's what real love is and it isn't something we should have to force, because it's automatically imprinted into our new nature. Does a dog have to force himself to bark?

We now are all baptized into one complete body (I Cor. 12:13), having obtained a new nature and leaving the old one behind. How else do you think we became sons of God?

You can't say that you're a new creature, but then prefer an all "black" church or an all "white" church. There is no color in Christ, because all he sees is the blood of his son.

We are all supposed to be born into

one body, but how did we get segregated?

Christ isn't denominational. It's only the division of men that keeps us separate in the church. So how can we all say we love the same God, but treat our own brethren differently and foul because they attend a different church than ours?

Being born again is a process that not only forces us to lose our previous identity, but it obligates us to claim the name of Christ.

There is no middle ground. Either you are in Christ or you're not.

The Wheat and the Tares

Can you recall the four conditions of the heart that I explained a few pages ago? Well, I'd like to go a bit deeper into that, so we can look at the "wheat" and the "tares".

Jesus spoke a parable concerning the kingdom of heaven, and how it was like a man that sowed good seed in his field…but while the good man was asleep, his enemy came and sowed tares among the wheat.

As the seeds grew tall, so did the tares. The servants of the good man wanted to go and pluck them up, but the good man decided against it, because if they were to root up the tares, they'd end up pulling up the wheat also.

So he decided to let both the wheat and the tares grow together until the harvest, then at that time, he would send his reapers to gather the tares, bind them and burn them.

Now, this is important for you to understand, because I'm going to show you exactly what this parable means and how it doesn't affect you.

When you see the word "wheat", it's referring to the believing Jews. The "tares" are referring to the unbelievers.

Matthew 13:38 reads, *"The field is the world; the good seed are the children of the kingdom; but the tares are the children of the wicked one."*

The enemy that sowed the evil seed was the devil. The harvest was the end of the world and the reapers were angels (vs.39).

God sent angels to cast out those that did iniquity. They were also thrown into a furnace of fire, where there was weeping and gnashing of teeth (vs. 41-42) & (Matt. 8:12).

He didn't take out the wheat, he just removed the tares and destroy them so the righteous can shine forth like the sun. If the bible says this, why do we believe otherwise?

People today are taught with the belief that there's going to be a "rapture" (which is not scripture), and when it happens, it will remove the righteous from the world and the wicked will be left behind…but the bible just said the wicked was removed and the righteous was left.

Can you see how religion can easily blind you if you don't hear the revelation of the word? We have been taught wrong for so long, that we honestly believe our church doctrine over the word.

If you were to look up the word "rapture", it's not even found in the bible. So where did we get that from? Churches refer to it to help explain the coming of the lord, and how we will all be changed in blink of an eye, but that's a false interpretation.

When you confess Christ, he comes in immediately, as in a blink of an eye. You are then changed instantly from darkness to light.

This what the bible means when it talks about a new heaven and a new earth. It's a new mindset and a glorified body, which is no longer connected to sin and corruption.

I Corinthians 15:51-58 talks about

being transformed from corruption to incorruption. It's how we are truly changed.

To be like him, we must put on immortality (2 Cor. 5:1-5) & (I Tim. 6:15).

Look at it this way, if you are waiting on Christ to come, then that only means that he's not here. If he's not here, how is he in you?

Why accept Christ into your heart if you don't truly believe he's there (Col. 1:26-29)?

People claim to belong to Christ, but their lifestyle is clearly evident that they don't believe he's is on the inside of them. This is why Christ becomes ineffective in their lives.

Rather than gaining a true revelation of the word, we'd rather hold on to our traditions and religion. If we did things by way of religion, we'd still see the lord as "the man upstairs".

Religion will blind you if you allow it. If we, the church, are blind to the truth, then those that are in darkness will never find their way.

2 Corinthians 4:3 says, *"But if our gospel be hid, it is hid to them that are lost."*

<u>Accepting Change</u>

Are you ready for change? If so, you must start by accepting the truth (Eph. 1:13).

The gospel of truth was given to one man in the whole bible, and that's Paul the apostle. To reject his teachings is to deny the gospel of truth.

It's mandatory that we stop lying to ourselves and ask God for a new nature.

If you are constantly away from the word, if you still act like the unsaved, if your life is the same way it was last year, then you need to admit that you need help and let God change you.

Religious people will never change. They believe they are doing everything correctly, but under a microscope, they are no different from those in the world.

This is the same spirit that was over the Pharisees and the Sadducees. They knew Jesus but didn't believe him. They were always against him, because they believed that their lifestyle was holy the way it was.

Change is important, because through change we find maturity. Through maturity we find the strength to accept responsibility, and when we can accept responsibility, God can do more with us, because he knows we won't go backwards.

When a frog is matured, he can still swim under water, but he can no longer live under water because he'll die. Tadpoles can't live on dry ground, because it will kill them.

When you come to Christ, he changes your nature. If your nature has changed, going backwards to your old life will kill you.

People that you once knew, who doesn't want God in their life, will never understand your change. Your" tadpole" friends will never see the world from your perspective, because their view is limited to their nature.

Chickens can never fly with hawks, just as caterpillars can never fly with butterflies. You may all exist together, but when your nature has changed, your destiny also changes, along with your purpose, your direction and your favor.

2 Corinthians 5:17 says, *"Therefore if any man be in Christ, he is a new creature: old things are passed away; behold, all things are become new."*

Chapter 7:
Doubt & Unbelief
Entered Into
The World

Chapter 7:
"Doubt & Unbelief Entered Into The World"
(7-A)

One of the greatest weapons that the enemy uses is to bring us into a state of doubt and unbelief.

Our whole foundation of Christianity is based on faith, so operating in unbelief can mean the difference between life and death. How can we be Christians if we don't believe?

Simplicity is in Christ. Then enemy comes to bring complex confusion. Salvation was made easy…only religion is complex.

How can you tell me that I can't come to church and receive the word unless I'm dressed a certain way? Is that your call to make? Who's really in control of the church?

When we allow ourselves to get caught up in church politics and not establish our foundation by saving souls, we are playing church. People can't find Christ if we are blocking their perspective of the truth.

If we aren't saving souls for God, then we are hindering them. They will perish because the "so-called" church kept them in unbelief through our double-minded lifestyle. Do you really want that kind of blood on your hands?

Remember what happened with Eve? She doubted the word of God, which led to the compromise her own purpose.

So what exactly is doubt? I'm glad you asked…

Doubt: *Uncertainty of mind; to waiver; to question God's word; to hesitate before believing God; not settling in surety; to move as a wave, tossed to and to and fro;*

When you don't walk after the spirit, your flesh will be in control. Aren't you aware that doubt and unbelief resides in the carnal mind?

The carnal mind is divided within itself. The bible calls this "double-mindedness". A man that is double-minded is unstable in all of his ways (James 1:8).

When you receive a bad report from the doctor, you have a choice to either believe what the doctor says, or you can believe what the word says concerning your healing. When you aren't sure what to believe, this is called wavering.

When you waiver, you are dealing with an issue of the mind. The understanding and wisdom of this carnal mind is sensual, earthly and devilish (James 3:15).

You cannot operate in both the spirit and the flesh. There's a war between the two and you will chose a side, just keep in mind that if you sow to the flesh, you'll reap corruption.

Matthew 6:24 says, *"No man can serve two masters: for either he will hate the one, and love the other; or else he will hold to the one, and despise the other. You cannot serve God and mammon."*

We don't like to think that we're double-minded or sowing to the flesh, but it's never intentional. This is how the enemy deceives us, because he allows us to think there's nothing wrong with our earthly mindset.

Truth is we need to do some spring cleaning. Renewing our mind, while cutting out some people from our lives…because when we engage with poor communication, it will corrupt our good manners (1 Cor. 15:33).

When you come to Christ, your entire

surroundings will start to change, because when you try to do good, evil is always present (Rom. 7:21).

The War Within

Within each of us is a battle between our flesh and our spirit. Our spirit wants to believe God, but when our flesh is too strong, it causes us to doubt God's word.

This is especially true with new believers, because they are the easiest to doubt God and wonder back into the lifestyle they once had. Why? Because after they come to Christ, they soon see that the church is full of other messed up people like them, so they leave.

Their image of a perfect church gets destroyed, so they stay home and attend Bed-Side Television. The problem with this is that they lose focus on what brought them to God in the first place.

The beginning of your spiritual walk will always be the hardest. This is why we need our Spirit to grow. Our flesh will be too strong in the beginning, but look at it as if it were a boxing match and you were the trainer…

Your fighter (your spirit man), is set for a title fight against the reigning champ (the flesh).

Every day is like a three-minute round, and the fight will only end in a decision when you die…winner takes all. In this case, your soul is the prize.

Being aware of the fight does not secure you a victory, only training and preparation can. When you feed your flesh, you give it control and the advantage to win. The same is true for your spirit.

Your spirit is guaranteed to win if you feed him. All he needs is the word. Constant meditation on Christ will sustain and preserve you.

When you get to a point where you can control your flesh and its random desires, then you can really tap into the deeper things of God.

In case you didn't know, no flesh can glory in his presence (1 Cor. 1:29), but did you know you can only worship him in spirit and in truth (John 4:21-24)?

God already knew there was nothing good in our flesh, so save the pity party for someone else.

Chapter 7:
"Doubt & Unbelief Entered Into The World"
(7-B)

As we reach the final segment of this book, I want to make sure I clear up a few things.

There is a difference between doubt and unbelief, because we are allowed to have doubts, but that doesn't make us unbelievers. Here's another definition for you...

Unbelief: *the failure to respond to God with trust; rejecting God's word; discrediting God;*

Unbelief is dangerous, because it completely contradicts your faith as a believer. In fact, it's so dangerous, that the Bible is completely against you being unequally yoked with someone who is an unbeliever!

2 Corinthians 6:14 says, "*Be ye not unequally yoked together with unbelievers; for what fellowship hath righteousness with*

unrighteousness? And what communion hath light with darkness?"

You must understand unbelievers have the spirit of unbelief, not faith. With that being said, what faith are you really of?

When you're an unbeliever, you can't accept the truth. When you deny the truth, you can't live right. Can you see why God called an unbeliever the "unrighteous"?

Remember a bit earlier when you read about a man's nature, both new and old? Here, the same rules apply. The unbeliever cannot act in faith to put his flesh under, because it's in his nature to live in sin.

As believers, we are no longer bound by the cords of sin, but it's still important that we put our flesh under submission on a daily basis (1 Cor. 9:27).

Everything you do, regardless if it's putting your flesh under, or believing God for something in particular, you need God's faith to do it.

Did you know that you can't even cast out devils when you don't have God's faith? Unbelief is the exact opposite of faith, just as faith is the remedy for unbelief.

<u>Your True Enemy</u>

We love to think that the devil is our enemy, but he was defeated already. He has no power, remember? He only has it if we give it to him.

Our flesh is our greatest enemy. It's not only the most dangerous to us, but it's the enemy we love the most (Gal. 5:17).

Isn't that crazy? We can't love the usher who frustrated us at church, but we pamper the one who plans to drag our souls straight to hell…unbelievable!

That type of behavior is built within our fleshly nature. In fact, when your flesh is operating in doubt and unbelief, you're almost guaranteed to panic at the first sign of trouble.

People only panic when they don't have a solution, hope or a way of escape. Well, how can you claim to have the spirit of Christ if you're not operating in faith? Anything that is not of faith is sin.

Did you know that Jesus' own disciples were guilty of unbelief?

In Matthew 8:24-27, it reads about how the disciples were on a ship in the midst of a storm. Although Jesus was on the ship with them, they believed the storm would overtake them.

They were not in faith, because they wavered, which is what most of us do today. When you make the decision to believe God on something, you have to trust him completely, otherwise you'll be giving place to the devil (Eph. 4:27).

When the bible tells you not to give place to the devil, do you really understand the reasons why? By now you should know better, because everything traces back to Adam.

Adam was given power and dominion over everything, right? But the devil wanted that power. The only way he could take that power from Adam, he had to get it through Eve, who was a type of Adam's soul.

Our flesh is our greatest enemy, because when we give the devil place, we allow him to take the power that Christ gave us. It's just sad because Christians never knew they had the power from the start.

Christ came to reclaim the power and dominion that Adam had lost. He then gave it to us, but since we don't realize what we have, we can never learn to truly appreciate it…so we give it away, just as Esau did with

Jacob.

Do not give your birthright away. All the promises in Christ are yes and Amen, but we need to realize that (2Cor. 1:20).

Then enemy will only come against your mind if you waiver in what you believe, just as he did with Eve.

No matter how tough the journey becomes, do your best to fight the good fight of faith!

"Fight the good fight of faith, lay hold on eternal life, whereunto thou art also called, and hast professed a good profession before many witnesses." – 1 Timothy 6:12

The Call To Salvation

This is the part of the book where you can have a chance to change your nature. With this simple prayer, you can be put into Christ, with no more worries of death, hell or the grave.

Once you say this prayer, you can close this book and walk away with a new type of confidence, knowing that everything that was lost by Adam is now rightfully yours again through Christ:

"I accept Jesus Christ as my lord and savior, because I believe that Jesus Christ is the son of God.

I believe that he died for my sins, was buried and rose again.

I also believe that my sins were paid for at the cross, so I can now live under grace rather than the law of sin and death.

Change my nature. Give me a new heart and renew my mind. Help me to be more sensitive to the Holy Spirit, so that my walk, my actions and my life can display your glory in everything I do.

...In Jesus' name, Amen."

Thank You for Reading!

For more information on Pastor Crump Sr. and the Door of Faith Ministries, visit:

www.DoorOfFaith.com

For more information on Epic Storm Publishing, visit:

www.EpicStormOnline.com